MUSICAL FORMS & TEXTURES

Musical FORMS & TEXTURES

A Reference Guide

by

Norman Demuth

Hon. R.A.M., Hon. A.R.C.M.,
Officier d'Académie, Professor of
Composition, Royal Academy of
Music, Member of the Sociétés
Internationales, Française et Belge
de Musicologie, Membre de Jury
du Concours du Conservatoire
National, Paris.

SALISBURY SQUARE · LONDON

79x
10

R 781.5
D399
cop3

REF
MT
58
.D4
1953
cir.

MADE AND PRINTED IN GREAT BRITAIN
BY CAMELOT PRESS LTD.
LONDON AND SOUTHAMPTON

FOREWORD

This little book does not pretend to be anything more than its title implies, but it is not a substitute for close and detailed study. It precedes the study of my four-volume *A Course in Musical Composition*[1] in which I have precluded and premised the introductory lessons in Form, Design, and Texture. The reader will find that the one book leads to the other, and that there is no question of overlapping, since the larger *Course* (which I envisage as a course of at least six years' duration for composers) pursues each point to its ultimate end. It is no less true than regrettable that a good many music students have neither time nor inclination to explore fully the hidden mysteries of musical form and design; but it is encouraging to find so many people interested in music (without any desire to pursue it as a career) who wish to get to the roots of things, and to find out concisely how composers draw up the "blue-prints" for their compositions. This book is intended for both students and amateurs. It goes further than those examination requirements which demand only the barest of bare bones in their most primitive and elementary states of growth.

Form has been presented too often entirely from the constructivist point of view, without sufficient emphasis on the expressive "reasons why". I have never been able to understand why, in certain examination papers, orchestral players should not be expected to know even the barest outlines of Fugue, Sonata, or Suite, pianists something about Concerto, Overture, and Symphony, and singers such things as melodic shape and rhythmic structure. Students take the line of least resistance in a busy and studious life without thinking of what they may be missing. They acquire a certain book knowledge within the prescribed limits of their particular subjects, but of the rest are content to remain in blissful ignorance. This ignorance accounts for much of the shapeless playing and singing one hears over and over again. Far too often a rubato is inserted where the composer has expressly stated that there should be none. This is spoken of smugly as "interpretation", regardless of the resultant distortion of the composer's

---

[1] Bosworth, 12s. 6d. per volume.

musical ideas. A wide knowledge of these basic ideas should eradicate this folly and those frequent lapses in judgment. However, to put this quite right would probably entail a complete revision of the curriculum and educational principles of this country.

I have avoided inserting charts and plans as far as possible, but complete avoidance has not been practicable. The reader should not be surprised at finding a large number of definitions, for musical form is not confined to symphonic designs. The subjects in each section are arranged alphabetically (with the exception of the first where it is not practicable to do so), thus making cross-reference quite simple.

I hope that the musical amateur will find it a stimulating guide for his thoughts. As I have said elsewhere, in several places, analytical listening is not the beginning and end of listening. It is but an aid to the full enjoyment of music; but analytical listening must be instinctive, and, if the basic knowledge is not there, this cannot be achieved, and enjoyment may well become a burden instead of a pleasure.

The examples have been chosen from works which are reasonably familiar and easily available, although occasionally I have mentioned some which may need some seeking. I have not given examples in every case, since sometimes the repertoire is too vast to make any choice adequate or necessary. The reader will not have to look far. Public libraries have good stocks of music, as a rule, although mostly confined to the established classics, but almost anything can be obtained on application.

NORMAN DEMUTH

Bognor Regis,
25.ix.52

CONTENTS

Form in Music serves to bring about comprehensibility through memorability. Evenness, regularity, symmetry, division, repetition, unity, relationship in rhythm and harmony and even logic—none of these elements produces or even contributes to beauty. But all of them contribute to an organisation which makes the presentation of the musical idea intelligible. The language in which musical ideas are expressed in tones parallels the language which expresses feelings or thoughts in words, in that its vocabulary must be proportionate to the intellect which it addresses, and in that the aforementioned elements of its organisation function like the rhyme, the rhythm, the meter (*sic*), and the subdivision into strophes, sentences, paragraphs, chapters, etc., in poetry or prose.

ARNOLD SCHOENBERG
"Brahms the Progressive", *Style and Idea*[1]

[1] Published by Williams and Norgate.

SYMPHONIC FORMS

FUNDAMENTALS Music is arranged in phrases and sentences which are themselves organised into forms. The same principles apply to every type of composition, from the simple hymn-tune to the elaborate symphonic movement.

PHRASES AND SENTENCES The length of the normal phrase is four measures, but this is only a generality and a starting-point. The phrase may be as short as two measures; this limit is rather too fine, and many authorities regard the two measures as a half-phrase. Composers have used phrases of three, four, five, six and even seven measures. Of these, the three and seven are the least common and the most awkward to handle. Phrases are not measured consistently throughout a work. The effect of this would be square and monotonous, and to avoid it phrases are extended in various ways. The conclusion of a phrase may be discovered by its cadence. When this is in doubt, the general shape of the music will indicate it—for there will be a natural tendency to take a breath, as it were. The end of a phrase is the equivalent of a colon: that of a sentence, a full-stop. Two phrases are regarded as constituting a sentence, the second, or responsive, phrase not necessarily being the same length as the first.
Phrases are extended by:

(1) The repetition of the whole phrase or a fragment of it, sometimes slightly widening the characteristic interval or otherwise varying it ornamentally.

(2) The sequential repetition of the whole phrase or a fragment of it. In both these processes, fragmentary repetition is the most frequent.

(3) Imitation in another part which temporarily holds up the progress of the phrase as a whole.

(4) Repetition of the whole cadence.

(5) Repetition of the final cadence chord.

(6) Delayed cadence by the insertion of an extraneous measure forming an extension somewhat similar to those in (1) and (2).

(7) Augmentation of cadence effected by lengthening the note-values so that those which normally occupy one or two measures now occupy two or four.

(8) By addition of a measure or measures, once a phrase has been established in its original rhythm.

A phrase-length can be determined quite easily: having found the cadence or breath mark, subtract all measures which come under the above headings, for these add length to the phrase without saying anything thematically fresh; the phrase will be the length of measures remaining, any extra ones constituting extensions.
Phrases may be contracted by:

(1) Overlapping—the first note of the second phrase commences at the same moment as the first one ends.

(2) Compressing a two-measure cadence into one so that it concludes on a weak instead of a strong beat.

The phrases and sentences are then organised into either Binary or Ternary Form.

BINARY FORM   A piece in two distinct sections. The first will terminate with a full close in the dominant. The second either introduces new material or treats the opening theme partially or completely in modulation and concludes on the tonic.

It is usually tabulated as A—B. (A. Say something. B. Say something else.)

EXAMPLES

Scarlatti's sonatas

TERNARY FORM   A piece in three distinct sections. The first will terminate in the tonic or dominant. The second will consist usually of new material leading to the dominant, but sometimes is founded upon fragments of the opening theme; this section is known as an episode,[1] since it appears only once and is a modulatory section. The third section is a repetition, or almost a complete repetition, of the first. It is usually tabulated as A—B—A. (A. Say something. B. Say something else. A. Refer to the first idea.)

The complete form is as follows:

A. Idea (subject or theme).
B. Episode.
A. Idea (subject or theme).

The repetition of the opening section gave rise to the expression "da capo", meaning "back to the beginning". This repetitive process, however, is not always literal, and composers from Beethoven onwards have frequently shown some invention in avoiding it. It was Arnold Schoenberg who advised students: "Never write what your copyist can compose for you", meaning that any copyist can copy an already existent passage into the full score.

This ternary (or three-idea) form governs almost all symphonic forms from their most primitive to their most elaborate conditions. It is found in its most general application in the Dance and in the Symphonic Minuet (or Scherzo), where it is combined with a movement called a Trio.

---

[1] The often-used term "episodical" is to be deprecated, as it is applicable to too many other forms of a wider scope than simple ternary, and is sometimes regarded as a useful short cut, since anything that contains an episode must of necessity be episodical, and this confuses issues to be discussed later.

MINUET AND TRIO The origin of the term "Trio" in this connection is slightly obscure, some maintaining that it was played by only three instruments, and others that as a dance it was performed by only three persons. Evidence supports the latter more than the former. The Trio is in exactly the same form as the Minuet, the sections of the dance tabulating themselves in this way:

Minuet	Trio	Minuet
A—Theme	A—Theme	A—Theme
B—Episode	B—Episode	B—Episode
A—Theme	A—Theme	A—Theme
A	B	A

The entire dance style, therefore, is a complete Ternary entity in itself and it will not confuse any issues to regard it as such. "A" in each section is repeated, likewise "B—A". In concert performance it is not usual, however, to make the repeats in the Second Minuet. The essential characteristic of the Trio is that it should be in absolute contrast to the Minuet. If the latter is chordal and pompous, the former should be graceful and lyrical, and vice versa. In the original dance Minuet and Trio, the Trio represented the wooing of a girl by two men, the girl behaving coquettishly and leading each one on in turn. The Scherzo is built on the same formal framework as the Minuet.

There are a great many short pieces, not necessarily in dance styles, which are in Minuet and Trio Form.

EXAMPLES

Minuets and Trios in Haydn, Mozart, and Beethoven symphonies

An extended use of Ternary Form can be found in the slow movements of some Sonatas and in ordinary "Piece for Piano, etc." In these examples the material is often "extended" in contrast with its extreme brevity in the Minuet and Trio. The original Ternary form was gradually expanded to serve as the basis of Sonata form.

SONATA FORM It has become customary to regard this as almost sacrosanct, a thing never to be disparaged and never to be altered. It is true that, fundamentally, it has sufficed composers up to the present day and looks as if it will outlive all of them; but even from its foundation only the most conservative composers have refrained from experimenting with it in various ways. Its influence is, as I have said, only fundamental, and authority for this experimentation can be found not only with those who established it, as it is known to-day, but with those who formulated it from the Ternary Germinal.

The term Sonata Form is a misnomer, since it can apply to the Sonata as a whole; I have often met with this confusion. If the Sonata as a whole were referred to as "the Sonata Manner", differentiation would be simple. Its other name, First-Movement Form, is no more explicit in detail, since many first movements are not written in it and it does duty for other types of composition. Certainly it is more satisfactory than Sonata Form because the majority of first movements are, indeed, written in it; but habits die hard and this one has become too well established to be discarded. Nobody has as yet found a better description.

Sonata Form emerged perfectly logically from the ordinary ternary idea, the original simplicity of the style growing gradually more complex. It grew through an extension of the Minuet style, the musical ideas becoming longer and the middle section, or Episode, freer both in material and key range. It was monothematic until the time of Carl Philip Emanuel Bach, when the bi-thematic principle appeared. This once more widened the scope of the design, and came to be tabulated thus:

A	B	A
Enunciation	*Middle Section*	*Recapitulation*
First subject in tonic key	Modulatory upon the material in the enunciation	First subject in tonic key
Connecting Episode or bridge passage		Connecting Episode or bridge passage
Second subject in dominant or some other related key		Second subject in tonic key
Codetta—ending in dominant key		Coda

Here we see the Episode acting as a modulatory flourish rather than, as formerly, a thematic interlude, and written with the sole purpose of modulating to the key of the Second Subject. Its range, therefore, is not as wide as that of the Minuet episode. The Middle Section presented imitative versions of the subjects, one against the other, passing through several related keys. It did not become a thematic Development Section until much later, but from the first has always been in the spirit of the Free Fantasia. The underlying principle was one of tonality and tonal relations. Composers were taught to think in this way and they conceived their ideas along tonal lines.

1. ENUNCIATION The elements constituting the Enunciation (it is better to use this term than that of "Exposition", for the purpose of the first section of Sonata Form is to announce the material, not to lay or place it out as is implied by the alternative title) have shown a steady expansion, and to-day the term "Subject" is almost another misnomer —certainly the words "First" and "Second" have lost their original significance. Originally the First Subject was so-called because it was

the principal one, the Second being subservient to it and of a different quality. To-day it is usually the Second which has more musical scope and resource, and the numerical differentiation applies solely to the order of presentation. The distinguishing feature of one subject has never been limited to a theme or thematic fragments, for some subjects are characterised by their rhythmic quality, and are, therefore, musical figures rather than themes. The one essential has been the contrast between the two; and consequently the original type of Second Subject was invariably short and less striking. Sonata form, therefore, was controlled entirely by the quality of the First Subject. In due course this emphasis changed, and Beethoven established the innovation of making the Form accumulative, the Second Subject taking on more scope and resource than the first, and dividing itself into several "parts", each of which had a definite theme or thematic rhythm. The term "Theme-Group" is more explanatory than "Subject".

The Subjects are connected by an *Episode* which lead from one key to another and bridge the tonal gap smoothly so that no aural shock takes place. From Beethoven onwards, it is often difficult to determine exactly where the Episodes start, but the best guiding factor is the final full close in the tonic key; there may be more than one full close, in which case the earlier ones will signal a repetition of the First Subject, particularly when the latter is complete. This applies only to tonal music; in the present century, when certain music no longer depends on tonal relations, it is frequently extremely difficult to decide where episodes begin except by instinct. In Symphonies and Concertos the orchestration helps considerably, but not so much as it does in determining the commencement of the Second Subject. The early basic modulatory passages usually concluded with an athematic figured flourish which established the new key beyond doubt. Beethoven removed the flourish and, having built his *Connecting Episodes* or *Bridge Passages* from the First Subject, led into the Second Subject smoothly and evenly.

The beginning of the *Second Subject* can still be decided by the cadence in the new key, after which the music takes on a new appearance. Tovey strenuously denied that the "look" of the thing had any part to play in distinguishing it. Experience has shown that although this may not be an ideal way of approaching the problem, since the tonal relation with the tonic key should be the deciding factor, the "look" of the music does give clear indication. In orchestral music the scoring will once more play a distinguishing part. If the First Subject is boldly rhythmic, for example, the Second will be melodically smooth, and vice versa. The question of masculinity *versus* femininity no longer applies, for if it did the Second Subject would always be feminine. Brahms, among others, proved the fallacy of this in his Fourth Symphony, where the clear-cut rhythm of the Second Subject is infinitely more masculine than the yearning suavity of the First.

The number of "parts" or themes in the "group" can be determined first by the cadences and then by the quality of what follows them. There may be any number of themes—the Second Subject of Beethoven's Piano Sonata in D, op. 10, No. 3, contains seven parts or themes; but this is exceptional.

The *Codetta* is easy to identify; in the music of the pre-Beethoven period it consists of another tonal flourish, while from Beethoven onwards it includes a reference to the opening music. Beethoven himself occasionally composed a new theme at this moment.

EXAMPLE

Sonata in F minor, op. 2, No. 1

In general, however, Beethoven reintroduced a fragment of the First Subject. The Enunciation closes in the dominant or some other related key, but never in the tonic, for the obvious reason that the latter would give an air of finality and thus make everything that followed redundant. An exception to this custom will be discussed later.

The double-bar-and-repeat always to be found in the music of the older classical composers is usually omitted to-day, both by composers, and by performers of those works in which it is included. Its purpose was to emphasise the ideas of the Enunciation, so that the interplay and variations of the material in the Middle Section could be followed more easily.

2. MIDDLE SECTION This can be called a Modulatory section, a Free Fantasia, or a Development section, according to the quality of the particular movement. This section is always longer in Symphonies and Concertos than in Sonatas, for the composer has the inexhaustible resources of the orchestra at his disposal; but although a skilled orchestral writer can always cover up deficiencies in inspiration and invention, his orchestral scoring cannot be a substitute for genuine musical creation. Although the composer here has ample scope for invention, if it is not expressive the music becomes merely a series of calculated sounds. There is no merit in cleverness by itself. It may be a section full of devices and processes, but if the result is not musical the work becomes like an attractively designed house with no roof. It is here that the greatest amount of skill is called into action, and this must be dictated by the expressive range of the music.

When the Middle Section is a *Free Fantasia* the composer can use any ideas which may come to him, without questioning their thematic relationship. This Schubert often did. Such a practice is usually described as loose thinking, and the section is somewhat pedantically criticised as being loosely formed.

It becomes a *Development Section* when it "presents the material in different ways", a usual, but not wholly accurate, definition, for this section of Sonata form. In the Symphonic Poem this section is used to develop the basic "story". Thus Tchaikowsky, in *Romeo and Juliet*, which is amongst the most complete in Programme Music, outlines the characters, and then in the Middle Section gives a musical description of the events and circumstances surrounding them. We know that a fight takes place, and we feel that the two principal characters are frustrated. The theme which signifies their love is primarily announced quietly and in this section acquires fire and passion whose intensity leaves no doubts. Similar parallels can be found in other Symphonic Poems.

It is in this section that technical device and process find their rightful place. The composer can twist his themes about as much as he likes, but it is only fair to say that few twist them about as much as many theorists maintain. Practically the whole resources of Variation are available, but it would be difficult to find a work in which total advantage is taken of them. The devices at the disposal of the composer in this section are:

Augmentation of theme.
Diminution.
Inversion.
Retrogression.
Change of Mode (change of key is hardly a developing device).
Change of Register—a theme may find added intensity by being placed
          on a 'cello instead of a clarinet, for example, this being the reverse
          of Mendelssohn's process in *The Hebrides* Overture.
Canon and Imitation.
Fragmentary treatment.

The last-named usually plays the most prominent rôle in a Development Section, the fragments being treated sequentially and imitatively. Modulation naturally takes place, but up to the time of Beethoven is restricted generally to related keys. Haydn's so-called Neapolitan changes, which strike the ear with great force and lift the music suddenly on to another plane, are still electrifying.

3. RECAPITULATION This presents all the material in the tonic key; hence there is often no need for a connecting Episode, which may be omitted or considerably shortened. The *Coda* brings the movement to a satisfactory conclusion. Its diminutive, Codetta, it will be remembered, served only to conclude the Enunciation.

In his Piano Sonata in D (K.284), Mozart reversed the order of events in the Recapitulation, and brought in the Second Subject before the First,[1] thus making the material balance each side of a musical archway, thus:

---

[1] The three "parts" of the Second Subject re-enter in the following order: Pt. 3, Pt. 1, and Pt. 2.

	Middle Section	→→→
Second Subject		Second Subject
Connecting Episode		Connecting Episode
First Subject		First Subject

In this way the musical ideas go up, over, and down, instead of downwards. It is a logical rearrangement, but has not become an established practice. César Franck used it in his Piano Trio in B flat, and in the present day it is used by Arthur Honegger. It is referred to as the "Façade Design".

Traditional tonal music requires to be controlled by a system of key-relationship. The chart of keys through which a Middle Section might roam, drawn up by the late Sir Frederick Gore Ouseley, Bart., the erudite theoretician and composer of the Victorian era, is as follows:

Major	*Minor*
Dominant	Relative Major
Dominant Minor	Minor of Relative Major
Supertonic	Subtonic (Minor 7th)
Mediant Minor	Submediant Minor
Tonic Minor	Flattened Tonic

Various modifications and adjustments crept into the Form, the most notable being that known as Modified First Movement Form. In scope this resembles the First Movement manner of C. P. E. Bach and his contemporaries. It is the most satisfactory design for a slow movement, the full form being far too resourceful for slow-moving music. The modifications are:

1. Slighter material.
2. No repeat of Enunciation.
3. Little, if any, Middle Section. In the first case it may amount to one modulatory chord, as in the Second Movement of Beethoven's Piano Sonata in C minor, op. 10, No. 1, the dominant seventh bringing the music straight back to the tonic.

Slighter material does not imply lighter material. The slow movement of Brahms's Fourth Symphony is in Modified First Movement Form, and the ideas are subjective and emotional.

The First Subject often subdivides itself into Ternary Form, and can be tabulated thus:

Enunciation	*Middle Section*	*Recapitulation*
First Subject in tonic	Limited, if existent	First Subject in tonic
(A) Theme		(A) Theme
(B) Episode		(B) Episode
(A) Theme		(A) Theme

(*Enunciation*)	(*Middle Section*)	(*Recapitulation*)
Connecting Episode		Connecting Episode
Second Subject in dominant or other related key		Second subject in tonic
Codetta		Coda

This modified version allows a single isolated piece to be written in a symphonic form, thus providing a counterpart in miniature to the greater Symphonic Poem in full First Movement Form.

RONDO   An expansion of First Movement Form grew out of an older design, which is neither Binary nor Ternary. This is the Rondo, Ronde, or Rondeau, whichever you wish. Of all nomenclatures it is the most satisfactory and convincing, for the main theme goes round and round Episodes, which, being Episodes, occur each only once.   The only formal strictures are that the main idea should appear at least three times, and that it should bring the movement to a close; otherwise the Rondo can continue indefinitely. It is the first of these strictures that sometimes leads people to regard the Rondo as a type of Ternary Form, but this is hardly justified. Rondo form is tabulated as follows:

A. Theme	C. Episode II
B. Episode I	A. Theme
A. Theme	

and so on.

From this, in combination with First Movement Form, grew what became known as Sonata Rondo Form, spoken of in certain books and in certain countries as "Grand Rondo". It combines the best of both worlds, and its structure is as follows:

Enunciation	*Middle Section*	*Recapitulation*
A. First subject in tonic	New material, forming	A. First subject in tonic
Connecting episode	Third subject	Connecting episode
B. Second subject in dominant or other related key	or Episode	B. Second subject in tonic
A. First subject in tonic		A. First subject in tonic
Codetta		Coda

The Sonata Form elements appear in the general layout of three main divisions, with two main subjects. The third division is a repetition or recapitulation of the first. The Rondo elements are seen in the repetitions of the First Subject, which appear immediately after any new statement. The First Subject becomes the main theme of the Rondo and it goes round and round the other thematic movements. Less

mechanical than Old Rondo, it forms a fitting design for the last movements of Sonatas and Symphonies; the original style of Rondo is found
mainly in Concertos.

Beethoven dropped the Sonata Scherzo, but he retained the Sonata-
Rondo Form. Sonata Rondo is not suitable for one-movement works.
For this purpose, First Movement (Sonata) Form remains the most
logical, especially when the work is based on the style known as
"cyclique".

CYCLIQUE This style, suggested by some early Italian composers
such as Vitali and Corelli and echoed to a small extent by Beethoven,
consists of building the entire work upon quotation and permutation of
the material appearing at the opening. For this purpose composers use
the Introduction to set out the basic germinals. The style is often
attributed to Liszt, but César Franck was pursuing it at the same time.
Saint-Saëns used it in his *Symphonie avec Orgue*.

The metamorphosis of themes, as the permutation principle is called,
was practised by Liszt in his Symphonic Poems, and by Franck to a
greater extent in his *Prélude, Aria et Final* for piano. His Symphony in
D Minor is based upon quotation of complete themes. The writer in
the First Edition of Grove's *Dictionary* suggested that Liszt found this
style a short cut to composition, as it did not require the composition
of numerous original themes, and thus saved time and trouble in a
busy life.

To say that this style is a short cut to composition is absurd. The
cyclique style is well established with modern composers. Advocated in
France by Vincent d'Indy, it was adopted by Debussy and Ravel in
their String Quartets. It has proved itself to be the logical style for
symphonic music, as it makes for complete continuity and cohesion.
To-day it is extraordinary to think that cyclique or non-cyclique was
almost a partisan battle-cry in the last century, so fiercely did composers regard the issue. The style suffers from mistaken identity,
inasmuch as it is often presumed to exist when the likeness is only
coincidental.

EXAMPLES

Prélude, Choral et Fugue (Franck)   Symphony in B flat (d'Indy)
Les Préludes (Liszt)   Piano Sonata (d'Indy)
Piano Sonata in B minor (Liszt)   Piano Sonata in C (Brahms), first
   and last movements

It is but fair to say that many authorities regard the term as meaning
a "cycle" of movements going round a series of tonal relationships, and
swinging from a tonic fulcrum. This is only one aspect of the style. It
may be reasonable, but it is not exactly accurate.

A great number of Symphonies written to-day proclaim their cyclique foundation and each forms an indivisible whole.

Sibelius's Symphonies grow from incidental cellules during the music, as if their composer had looked back to find a suitable germinal at each point in the work's progress. There is no initial setting out of all the ideas.

VARIATION   This is the art of presenting a theme in different ways by amending or decorating it so that eventually it becomes unrecognisable but yet is always present. It is not so much a form as a process, but since it embraces such styles as Ground, Chaconne, and Passacaglia, it takes on some formal features. It is the earliest form of musical design, and is to be found in its most primitive state in Gregorian music, when the plain Intonations and Prefaces are sung to elaborate florid music.

Variations themselves fall under two headings:

> 1. Air with Variations (Air Varied)
> 2. Symphonic Variations

1. This style consists of separate and complete studies on the theme.

2. A continuous commentary upon the theme, in which the music comes to no conclusions until the final cadence.

Variation falls into three categories:

> 1. Ornamental
> 2. Decorative
> 3. Amplified

1. ORNAMENTAL   The composer displays his ingenuity by twisting the theme into many shapes. In addition to the processes mentioned under the Middle Section of Sonata Form, the theme can undergo:

Change of time-signature.

Change of harmony.

Change of character achieved as a result of the above.

Contrapuntal treatment, which may make the theme the subject of a
    Fugue, or may subject certain elements of it to canonic, fugal,
    or imitative treatment.

Change of shape through the addition of other notes.

2. DECORATIVE   The theme remains practically unaltered, but is decorated by changes of harmony and counterpoint, and appears in other voices besides that of the original.

3. AMPLIFIED   The theme is distended and distorted beyond recognition, the composer's fancy taking him off at tangents suggested by certain melodic fragments of the theme.

Variations can be illustrated by the finest and by the most banal music in existence. Virtuoso pianist-composers used to write sets of

"Variations brillantes" for themselves to play, based on well-known themes of which "God Save the King" did duty on quite a number of occasions. Such masterpieces need not be quoted here; the following list will be found to be representative of all three categories.

EXAMPLES

The Carman's Whistle (Byrd)

Goldberg Variations (Bach)

(So-called) *Harmonious Blacksmith* (Handel)[1]

Variations in F minor (Haydn)

Piano Sonata in A—(K.331) (Mozart)

Piano Sonata in A flat, op. 26 (Beethoven)

Air and Variations in B flat (Schubert)

Variations sérieuses (Mendelssohn)

Études Symphoniques (Schumann)

Variations on a Theme of Handel (Brahms)

Variations Symphoniques (César Franck)

Istar (d'Indy)

Don Quixote (Strauss)

Enigma (Elgar)

OVERTURE   There are two varieties:

1. Operatic
2. Concert

In due course a certain formal union took place, but in the first place the term was applied to what eventually became known as Symphony.

1. The early OPERATIC OVERTURE was not intended to be listened to with any serious intention. It served to get the audience seated and reasonably quiet, and brought animated conversation to a close. The two original designs were those used by Scarlatti and Lully.

The difference can be seen as follows:

Italian	*French*
A quick movement	A slow strong rhythmic Introduction
A slow movement	leading into
A quick movement (played without a break)	A quick Fugato
	A slow movement, often simply the repetition of the opening Introduction in part or whole

Certain variations crept in with the French style, the final slow section either consisting of new material or being omitted altogether. Of the two styles, it is the more popular, there being something truly magnificent about the opening summons to attention. Not only did this style lead directly into the later Symphony, but it appeared in certain Suites as the first movement.

---

[1] It is possible that Handel may have heard a blacksmith whistle this tune, but it is of French origin and differs slightly from Handel's version. It is sung in France to the words "*Plus ne suis ce que j'ai été*", a Chanson by Clément Marot dated 1532.

EXAMPLES

Italian　　　　　　　　*French*

Saul (Handel)　　　　Suite in D (Bach)

The classical Overture of Mozart came into the category of a movement in Sonata Form, with an Introduction in most cases, and dramatic episodes in the middle referring to some situation in the Opera itself.

EXAMPLES

Don Juan

Die Zauberflöte

This was continued and extended by Beethoven.

EXAMPLES

Leonora, No. 3

Coriolan

While composers before Beethoven sometimes used themes from the opera in the overture, it was Beethoven who established the idea which reached its romantic conclusion in Weber.

EXAMPLES

Oberon

Der Freischütz

Wagner established the form as a Symphonic force, the Overture to *Tannhäuser* being the first complete example of this use. It foreshadowed situations in the story rather than illustrated the mood, as in Weber, or utilised the material as in Beethoven. From this moment the Overture became almost a complete résumé of the Opera.

The French Opéra-Comique composers used the main themes more or less in Sonata Form, introducing one extra theme which, by interrupting the flow of ideas, formed a kind of dramatic episode.

EXAMPLE

Le Roi l'a dit (Delibes)

An easy way of getting over the difficulties lies in the Pot-Pourri Manner which consists of a string of themes from the Opera without any formal or thematic connections.

EXAMPLES

William Tell (Rossini)

Carmen (Bizet)

This type of Overture was not intended to be taken at all seriously, and although both the above examples brought the main ideas to light, it did not matter very much if nobody listened; Rossini was fully aware of this!

The Operatic *Prelude* serves more to set the atmosphere of the drama than to provide a résumé.

EXAMPLES

Lohengrin (Wagner)
Parsifal (Wagner)

However, in the so-called Prelude to *Die Meistersinger* Wagner did indeed write a complete résumé of the work. The description is justified by the fact that it runs straight into the First Act. In scope and resource, in technical mastery and range of expression, this Prelude is the greatest Operatic Overture ever as yet composed.

2. A single-movement work in Sonata Form, the CONCERT OVER-TURE comes in the category of Programme Music. It either tells a story or paints a landscape. It is sometimes called a "Fantasy-Overture".

EXAMPLES

The Hebrides (*Fingal's Cave*) (Mendels-sohn)

Carnival Overture (Dvořák)
A *Faust Overture* (Wagner)

It differs from the Symphonic Poem by being shorter and not quite so detailed; but the dividing line is sometimes difficult to distinguish. However, it would be impossible to describe Strauss's *Don Juan* or *Ein Heldenleben* as anything but Symphonic Poems and Mendelssohn's *Hebrides* as anything but a Concert Overture.

CONTRAPUNTAL TEXTURES

CANON A type of composition in which the voices enter one after the other in strict imitation, interval for interval, of the first voice at different pitches. It is the most learned of all types of composition, and at one time served as the equivalent to the modern crossword puzzle, composers writing Canons as a pastime. Beethoven was an inveterate writer of Canon, while Haydn had a canonic visiting card. There are two kinds of Canon:

1. Finite
2. Infinite or Perpetual

1. FINITE Here the voices stop at a given point and the piece is of a premeditated length.

EXAMPLE

Two-Part Inventions (Bach)

2. INFINITE OR PERPETUAL The voices repeat the tune, in turn, over and over again in strict Canon until someone gives the signal to stop. Such a Canon is known as a "Round" because the music goes literally round and round the singers or players and there is no reason for it to stop this side of Eternity.

EXAMPLES

"Sumer is icumen in" (John of Reading)
"Three Blind Mice"

Canon may be in any number of parts or voices, and may be vocal or instrumental (in both cases the entries are spoken of as "voices"). It may be a separate piece in itself, in which case it is often called an "Invention", or it may be simply an isolated and incidental passage in a work. The Georgian Church composers were very adept at introducing this texture in odd places during the settings of the Daily Offices. Canon is not the same as Imitation. Canon must be exact repetition and talk about "strict" and "free" Canon, meaning that the repetition need not be exact, begs the question. If the repetition be not exact, the piece is imitative and not canonic.

Canon is described by certain qualifying numbers. Thus "Canon 2 in 1" means a Canon for two voices upon a single theme. "Canon 4 in 2" a four-voice one with two themes, these being introduced simultaneously and alternated between the voices.

The voices may enter at any interval between each other, the most usual being the unison, the octave, the fourth, fifth, and ninth. The first voice is known as "Dux" (Leader) and the others "Comes" (Companion—and in the plural "Comites").

Canons are of several quantities:

1. CANON BY AUGMENTATION   When the Comes sings the theme in notes of longer value than the Dux.

Ex. 1   Bach: The Art of Fugue

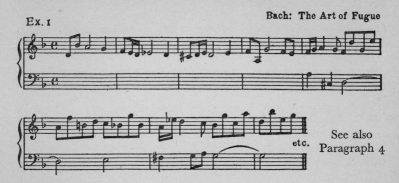

See also
Paragraph 4

2. CANON BY DIMINUTION   When the Comes sings the theme in notes of shorter value than the Dux.

Ex. 2   Bach: The Art of Fugue

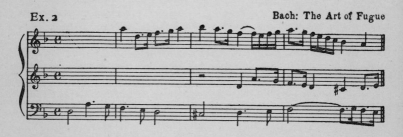

3. CANON CANCRIZANS   When the Dux and Comes start together, the latter singing the former backwards. This is an entirely erroneous description, as crabs move sideways, but it is a relic of the past, born in ignorance, and has remained ever since. Pedantic names for it are *Canon Recte et Retro*, *Canon Rectus et Inversus*, and *Retrograde Canon*, the last being the most explanatory. The old composers prided themselves upon their Canon Cancrizans, seeing in it a sure sign of technical mastery. This, indeed, it may be, but the ear which can detect and follow the process must be even more highly skilled. Still more so must it be to follow the theme backwards and recognise it, since it becomes virtually a new one. The effect, therefore, is optical rather than aural. (Ex. 3.)

4. CANON BY INVERSION   When the upwards and downwards progress of the Dux is contradicted by the Comes. (See Ex. 1 and 2.)

Ex. 3   Bach: Musical Offering

5. CANON PER ARSIN ET THESIN Although applicable to Canon by Inversion, it also implies a canon in which the notes of the Dux appearing on strong beats appear on weak in the Comes.

6. CANON BY CONTRARY VALUES A combination of Diminution and Augmentation. The long notes in the first voice become short in the second and vice versa. In this way the open note-heads are filled-in in the first case and the filled-in become open in the second. This results in a complete deformation of the theme, and it becomes unrecognisable.

Ex. 4   Bach: The Art of Fugue

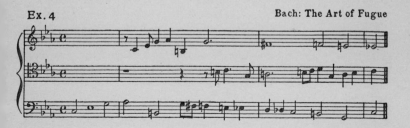

A certain confusion sometimes becomes apparent in the minds of students as to the difference between inversion and retrogression, which it may be as well to clear up here. Inversion refers to the contradictory rise and fall of the notes between Dux and Comes. In retrogression the

notes of the theme are written out by starting at the last and working backwards to the first.

FUGUE   A contrapuntal work based upon a theme (called the Subject) which is treated imitatively in accordance with certain established customs. Although it falls into a definite framework, it is not a Form. The word "Fugue" means "flight", in French, and is used in its literary context in ordinary conversation. In French history books Louis XVI is described as having *fait la fugue* from Paris to Varennes.

Fugues are of two kinds, the Classroom and the Composer's Fugues. The former insists upon certain exigencies which place the texture upon the highest level of technical skill, the actual *musical* result being, seemingly, of secondary importance. Many noted theorists have set down all the things which should happen in every Fugue, but composers have always followed their own dictates. It is impossible to align No. 1, Book One, of Bach's *Forty-Eight*, for example, and many others, with the dictates of the theorists. At one time it was not regarded as a musical expression and was used solely as a mental exercise. The departure of the *Forty-Eight* from the theorists' "rules" made their work anathema in many places, notably at the Paris Conservatoire, whose then Director, Cherubini, had written a learned and exceedingly dull treatise on Fugue and, consequently, would not tolerate any composer's works which denied the principles he strenuously upheld. Charles Gounod was told that he could either destroy his copy of the *Forty-Eight* or leave the Conservatoire; he was certainly never to bring it inside the building.

The fundamentals, however, have remained the same for all, and composers have treated the texture in the same way as they have treated Sonata Form by bending its basic principles to their will.

Fugue is ternary in design, its main sections being the Exposition, Middle Section, and Final entry of the Subject, usually in the tonic. Since the Exposition is not repeated *in toto* at the end, many authorities maintain that it is in binary design, the final entry of the subject being merely the moment of the final return to the tonic. It is, therefore, a matter of opinion; the writer leans to the ternary idea.

The Exposition is not simply to announce the subject; otherwise it might consist of but a few notes. It is for the purpose of placing- or laying-out the voices. These enter one after the other, the odd numbers, who sing the Subject, being answered at another pitch by the even, who sing the Answer. The voices may enter in any order—i.e. in a SATB[1] Fugue the succession need not be SATB. The constituent fundamental elements of the Exposition are the Subject, Answer, Counter-Subject, Free Part. These are laid out as follows:

---

[1] Soprano, Alto, Tenor, Bass—the term "voices" implying the several "parts" whether vocal or instrumental.

Subject...Counter-Subject...Free Part..........................
   Answer..........Counter-Subject....Free Part.........
      Subject............Counter-Subject...
         Answer..........

Certain additions and interpolations appear in this basic Exposition from time to time. These include a short passage, sometimes only two or three notes, which joins the re-entries of the Subject or the Answer to the Counter-Subject. This is quite wrongly called the Codetta; but it brings nothing to a close, and Link would be the better term. It occurs when the fancy of the composer takes him beyond the limits of the theme in question, or when the Counter-Subject has not made a completely balanced entity at the moment the other voice finishes.

It will be noticed that each voice has been heard with the Counter-Subject except the first, and that each voice has "sung" the Counter-Subject except the last. To obviate this, there is sometimes a Redundant Entry of the Subject on the voice which first announced it, so that it may be heard with the Counter-Subject, the latter being sung by the last voice to enter.

Sometimes, but very rarely, there is a Counter-Exposition in which those voices who originally had the Subject now sing the Answer, and those who had the Answer, now sing the Subject. The order of entry of the voices is often in reverse or in some different order.

Such is the general plan of the Fugal Exposition, which ends the moment the last entry of Subject or Answer has concluded, the music forthwith changing to something else, although that "something else" may be fragmentarily connected with the Subject.

SUBJECT This is one of three qualities and four quantities. The qualities are:

1. Andamento—A Subject which is a complete melodic and rhythmic phrase in itself.

2. Soggetto—This is short and contains some characteristic interval which becomes significant as the Fugue progresses.

3. Attacco—Simply an athematic figure.

1. ANDAMENTO *Organ Fugue in G minor (Bach)*. This is in one continuous phrase, but it has considerable rhythmic contrast.

No. 24, Book One ("Forty-Eight"). This is smooth throughout, and although it has some characteristic intervals which suggest ways of expansion, its length is such that it cannot be a real Soggetto. It may be regarded as a series of appoggiaturas, or a succession of leaps of the diminished seventh. In either case there are ample opportunities for fragmentary treatment.

No. 10, Book Two ("Forty-Eight"). A subject of considerable variety in three distinct sections.

No. 20, Book One (*"Forty-Eight"*). A two-section Andamento.

2. SOGGETTO This is more common than Andamento. A typical example is: *No. 5, Book One* (*"Forty-Eight"*)

The next two examples suggest that there may be a definite melodic impulse behind the Soggetto.

No. 16, Book One (*"Forty-Eight"*)
"St. Ann" Fugue for Organ (*Bach*)

Extreme brevity is found in:

No. 22, Book One (*"Forty-Eight"*)
No. 9, Book Two (*"Forty-Eight"*)

Sometimes there is an element of doubt as to which quality a Subject really belongs.

No. 3, Book One (*"Forty-Eight"*). Here the harmonic basis as distinct from any melodic impulse suggests that, despite its length, this is Soggetto rather than Andamento.

Many Andamento subjects include Soggetto elements:

No. 15, Book One (*"Forty-Eight"*)
No. 20, Book One (*"Forty-Eight"*)

3. ATTACCO Although terse, it may consist of more than one figure.
No. 10, Book One (*"Forty-Eight"*). This includes the arpeggio figure of the opening bar and subsequent "Alberti" treble.
No. 19, Book One (*"Forty-Eight"*) and *No. 3, Book Two* (*"Forty-Eight"*) are self-explanatory.

A two-figure Attacco need not be in notes of equal length:

No. 20, Book Two (*"Forty-Eight"*)

In can be sequential in interval:

No. 5, Book Two (*"Forty-Eight"*)

or purely rhythmic:

No. 16, Book Two (*"Forty-Eight"*)

It is rare that all three types appear in one subject. The next may be regarded as a combination of Soggetto and Attacco—the former because of its brevity, and the latter since the repeated leaps of a sixth make it a figure more than a characteristic interval.

No. 3, Book One (*"Forty-Eight"*)

There are others, and it must be repeated that very often it is a matter of personal opinion as to which type a subject may conform.

The Four Quantities are:

1. SIMPLE The subject is contained within the limits of tonic and dominant, i.e. a fifth up and a fourth down.
2. DERIVED The subject exceeds the above limit.

3. CONCLUSIVE The subject ends on the tonic.

4. INCONCLUSIVE The subject ends on the dominant. (The French term for this is *suspensif*.)

1. The limitations of a SIMPLE Subject are such that it cannot be Andamento. Two not previously quoted are:

No. 4, Book One ("*Forty-Eight*")
No. 9, Book Two ("*Forty-Eight*")

2. It is unnecessary to quote examples of DERIVED Subjects, as their name is legion.

3. A good instance of an extended CONCLUSIVE Subject is:

Organ Fugue in G minor (Bach)

and that of a short one:

"*St. Ann*" *Fugue (Bach)*

4. The INCONCLUSIVE Subject is in some cases problematical and in others obvious, as in:

No. 3, Book Two ("*Forty-Eight*")

It usually happens that the Subject and Counter-Subject overlap, and it is seldom that a Subject can be said to end on the beat or a fraction of the beat immediately before the succeeding voice enters with the Answer.

The first essential of a good Fugue Subject is a certain pithiness and sense of musical shape, no matter what the quality and quantity. The number of times the interval of the diminished seventh is used increases as Fugue progresses through history. No other interval has proved itself so fertile in Fugue, and in this respect it equals the fertility of the superimposed rising fourths which appear so often in Symphony.

The early rule for a Fugue Subject held that it should not exceed the compass of an octave. Bach's complete indifference to this stricture was one of the reasons which made the schoolmasters say that he was "wrong" and caused them to place the veto mentioned above on the *Forty-Eight*.

ANSWER The Fugue Subject is answered by the next voice in the dominant. It is an abiding rule that whenever they appear in the Subject, the tonic and dominant must be answered by the dominant and tonic respectively. This means that there must be two kinds of Answer, one which transposes the Subject a fifth higher or a fourth lower, interval for interval, and one which has to turn the upward leap into a fourth and the downward one into a fifth. These Answers are called Real and Tonal.

1. REAL ANSWER This is a literal transposition of the Subject. It is used when the Subject does not range as high as a perfect fifth from the tonic, or when it goes outside that interval without touching the dominant.

(*See Ex. 5(a), p. 22.*)

2. TONAL ANSWER This is an inexact transposition of the Subject. It is used when the Subject modulates or when it touches the dominant. At this point the second voice will be a fourth higher (or fifth lower) when it answers the tonic, *but* everything else will be the normal fifth higher (or fourth lower). Two exceptions are found when the Subject moves scalewise through the Dominant or consists of the tonic chord played arpeggio-wise. In the former case the Answer moves by step in order to avoid the repetition of one note; in the latter the actual dominant arpeggio preserves the essential character of the Subject.

Generally speaking, there are more Tonal Answers than Real ones.

(See Ex. 5(b).)

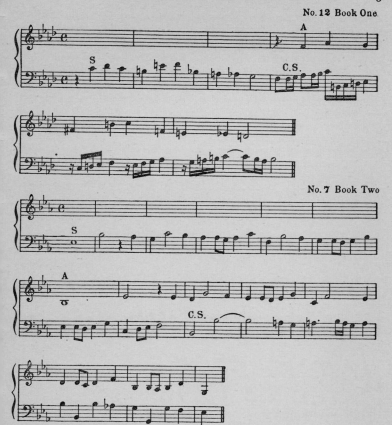

COUNTER-SUBJECT As its name implies, this is a theme which runs "counter" or against the Subject, and it is sung by each voice in turn so that another parallel melodic line is added to the texture. It would appear to be perfectly reasonable and logical for the text-books to insist upon it appearing on each occasion, thus requiring it to be in double or invertible counterpoint; this means that it can "go" both above and below the Subject or Answer. When this happens, it is called a "Regular" or "Real Counter-Subject"; but Bach did not always observe those conditions, and on such occasions each entry is called "*a* counter-subject" as distinct from "*the* counter-subject".

FREE PART Whereas the text-books insisted upon the Counter-Subject being in double or invertible counterpoint, the melodic line immediately following the Counter-Subject has always been freely written and need not be the same on each occasion. Hence the term Free Part. Doubtless an excessively erudite and mathematical mind could make it "go" each side of Subject and Answer if he wished, but this is unnecessary. One objection would be that it would add an extra important line to the texture and if it were considered a Counter-Subject, would be inordinately long in the first place and incomplete in each succeeding one. One feels sure that the freedom was not granted as a concession to the student.

The last voice having concluded the Subject or Answer, whichever it may be, for in an odd-numbered vocal design it must necessarily be the Subject which appears last—and there being neither Redundant Entry nor Counter-Exposition, the music moves on to the Middle Section.

MIDDLE SECTION So far the music has consisted of repetitions of the Subject and its corresponding Answers in the tonic and the dominant. As it is impossible to continue in this way, the Fugal Middle Section modulates from key to key so that the theme may be heard at various tonal levels. In order to do this, passages called Episodes are written. It is by these means that the music modulates to whatever key in which the theme is to reappear; Cherubini drew up the following range of keys:

Major	*Minor*
Dominant	Mediant
Sub-mediant (Minor)	Dominant (Minor)
Sub-dominant	Sub-mediant
Supertonic (Minor)	Sub-dominant
Mediant (Minor)	Subtonic (Flattened Seventh)
Dominant	Tonic

The Episodes also break the monotony of unceasing Subjects and Answers. Each Episode is usually founded upon a fragment of the Subject, and the student must not be led astray by seeing what he takes to be a re-entry of the Subject, for at second glance he will see that it is an Episode based on a fragment of it. An example of this can be found in No. 2, Book One, of the *Forty-Eight*. The modulations will be to closely-related keys.

The Subject is not necessarily treated literally at each repetition. It may appear in Augmentation, Diminution, Inversion and even Retrogression, although this is extremely rare. It may also appear in what is known as Stretto.

STRETTO Literally, this is a drawing together of the voices. Instead of entering at the conclusion of the Subject, the voices overlap and enter at various distances from each preceding one. It is not absolutely necessary, according to the *Forty-Eight*, that they enter at the same distance in turn. There are two kinds of Stretto:

1. PARTIAL   When not all the voices take part—*not* when only part of the Subject is used.

2. COMPLETE   When all the voices are so engaged.

The finest example of continuous stretti can be found in No. 1, Book One, of the *Forty-Eight*, which is a so-called "Stretto Fugue"; there are no Episodes and, therefore, it has no true Middle Section. Example 6 shows good illustrations of stretti.

FINAL ENTRY   Finally, the Subject enters for the last time, usually in the tonic, always so in the classroom variety, but not always in the composer's style. It is quite likely that Stretti will be met with at this point. The Classroom Fugue insists upon it, but composers find that it is preferable to indulge this fancy in the Middle Section. The scholastic idea is to tie everything up at the end, the voices almost tumbling over each other in their anxiety not to be left out. Such a practice, amounting to a recapitulation of the Exposition, would emphasise the ternary nature of Fugue. The Fugue concludes with a Coda often founded upon a Pedal Point; sometimes the Coda consists of an extra statement of the Subject forming a repeat of the "official" Third Section.

Fugue has come to be regarded as a deadly serious business, demonstrative only of erudition and calculated precision. The real Composers' Fugue is anything but this. The contrapuntal textures are capable of infinite variety, from solemnity to frivolity, and Fugue contains a good many examples of the scherzo spirit. It is the custom to invite candidates for University Degrees to write a Fugue in three hours, thus making it a kind of handicap race. Contrapuntal facility is no merit in itself, although extremely useful. A friend of the writer prepared himself for this hurdle race by writing a Fugue in three hours every day for two months. He felt himself quite capable of writing a Fugue, but the time limit required a course of training. Since then he has never written another.

Ex. 6   No. 8 Book One

Answer treated in stretto.
II – Rhythmic alteration of Answer in augmentation.
III – Partial entry of Answer, varied.

c

No. 9 Book Two

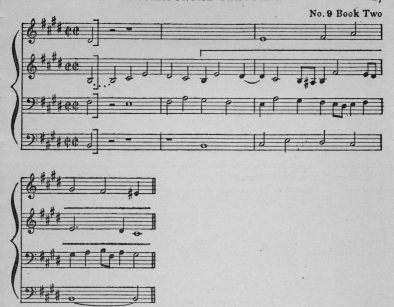

ACCOMPANIED FUGUES These are found mainly in Ora-torios. The orchestral part adds to the choral textures without doubling all the voice parts. Bach and Handel were supreme masters of this art.

DOUBLE FUGUE A Fugue with two Subjects. These may be treated in two ways.

1. They may be announced separately in full Exposition, and then combined.

2. They may be combined from the very first. In this case some authorities regard the Second Subject as a Counter-Subject; but this alters the original position of the Counter-Subject in the scheme of things, since it will thus enter before the conclusion of the Subject.

EXAMPLES

Fugue in C minor (on a theme of Legrenzi) for Organ (Bach)
Fugue in B minor (on a theme of Corelli) for Organ (Bach)

TRIPLE FUGUE A Fugue with three Subjects, treated in the above alternative ways. The "St. Anne" Fugue for Organ of Bach is sometimes considered a Triple Fugue because it is in three main sections, although the Subject in the second section does not reappear in the third.

EXAMPLE

Sonatina for Organ (Karg-Elert)

FUGATO A movement or passage in fugal style which may not adhere to all the requirements of Fugue, although it neither precludes nor insists upon observance of them. It often helps a composer over a difficult moment when inspiration fails and recourse has to be made to technical device.

FUGHETTA A Fugue on a small scale, whose subject is limited in scope and whose middle section is short, the key-range being restricted to those few closely related to the tonic. It holds the same relation to Fugue as that held by Sonatina, Sinfonietta, and Concertino to their respective counterparts.

IMITATION The copying of one voice in another, not interval for interval, but preserving the original contour. If, for example, the original part progressed C—G—F, the imitating voice could follow it C—A—G, and this would be considered sufficiently imitative, even if the second voice dropped to F instead of G. Some authorities consider it as "free canon", but this is a paradox.

RICERCARE An Italian term meaning "to seek out". It was a primitive style of Fugue much used by Frescobaldi and his contemporaries. It did not conform to any fugal exigencies, and the Subject could be answered at any pitch without reference to tonal questions. A modern idea of the style has reproduced its principles as a set of Variations. These "search out" the potentialities of the opening Ostinato theme to their utmost capacity.

EXAMPLE

Ricercari for Piano (Mihalovici)

It may be mentioned here that the Czech composer and teacher Antonin Reicha, who had Berlioz, Liszt, Franck, and Gounod in his class at the Paris Conservatoire, strenuously denied the strictures of the theorists, and wrote a number of Fugues which answered the Subject interval for interval at any pitch. He regarded Fugue purely as a contrapuntal texture, and made use of all the fugal processes. This point of view was revolutionary then, and would be so considered now. The attitude was explained away by a writer in the original Grove's *Dictionary* as being a direct reversion to the principles of the Ricercare and having no connection with Fugue as such.

DANCE STYLES

ACTE DE BALLET A one-act entertainment based upon a story sung throughout as in a one-act opera, with dancing and mimed commentaries dependent upon the action and progress of the plot. It forms a shortened version of the Opéra-Ballet, with the qualification that the ballet takes pride of place and is, indeed, the *raison d'être* for the whole. Rameau wrote several "Actes de Ballet", among which may be mentioned *Pygmalion* and *La Naissance d'Osiris*.

ADAGIO The high-light in a Ballet, the equivalent of the Concerto-Cadenza. The Ballerina shows off her prowess, supported by the male dancer who hovers discreetly in the background, assisting her in her elevations. Unlike the Concerto-Cadenza, however, it is more concerned with beauty of movement than with brilliance of technique. The music on these occasions is often insignificant in order not to detract attention from the Ballerina.

ALLEMANDE Accurately speaking, this is not a dance style, but it appears in dance suites, sometimes taking the place of the Prelude. It is written in equal semi-quavers, in common time, and commences with a crisp anticipation of the first note of the first complete bar, the effect being similar to a *rat-tat* on a door.

BALLET A stage play in which the story is unfolded by means of dancing and miming. Originally consisting of dance styles as they appear in the early dance suites, it became an entity distinct from its operatic connections in the time of Lully and particularly during the time of Rameau.

The score is divided up into separate movements, each extremely short owing to the limited physical endurance of the human body. During the present century, however, there has been a tendency to overstep this traditional framework and create ballets whose continuity is as marked a feature as was its original sectionalism. Classic examples of this are Ravel's *Daphnis et Chloë*, and Stravinsky's *Petrouchka* and *Le Sacre du Printemps*.

Attempts have been made to "dance" Symphonies. Brahms's Fourth (*Choreartium*) and Tchaikowsky's Fifth (*Les Présages*) are memorable examples; but, owing to the limitations and absence of continuity in the dancer's technique, these were not altogether satisfactory. The best ballets are those set to special music. Among the classics may be mentioned *Les Sylphides*, danced to a string of pieces by Chopin, and *Carnival*, to Schumann's piano work of the same name.

Classical Ballet is romantic, the standard work of its kind being *Giselle*, by Adolphe Adam. Among modern works to specially composed music, one must mention *The Three-cornered Hat* (Manuel de Falla), *The Miracle of the Gorbals* (Sir Arthur Bliss), and *Horoscope* (Constant Lambert). Vaughan Williams's *Job* is described as "A Masque for Dancing".

Owing to the prevalent taste in that country, Ballet at one time became closely associated with Russia, and the spectacular ballets of Tchaikowsky and Glazounov, particularly the former's *Sleeping Princess*, formed a style comparable to spectacular opera popular in the middle of the last century.

Ballet creation is a collaboration between scenario writer, choreographer, composer, and scenic artist. Although many famous works have been created round music not composed for this medium, the ideal lies in the active co-operation of these four individuals. Actual creation is often done round a table, mainly between choreographer and composer. The latter is slightly subservient to the former and has to fall in with requirements which he seldom understands. Consequently, he may be driven to exasperation by the ever-changing whims of the choreographer, who will calmly demand either the addition of any number of bars on a certain rhythm and equally calmly require the composer to destroy a whole page or pages after their composition; but this is the fun of the game, and its sweet reasonableness is evident in the successful performance. The music should match the movement. When the dancers are scurrying about, the music should do likewise; when the dancers are moving gracefully and slowly, the music should move with them, sustaining the movement—music for ballet must never be static. Unfortunately, this match is not always so arranged, and the results are incongruous, the orchestra giving an impression of intense life and activity while the dancers stand quite still, and vice versa. If the choreographer is sensitive to music, this will never occur.

From the purist's point of view, it is altogether wrong for a choreographer to hear some music and decide to dance it, and for a composer to say, "Here is my music; dance it."

BALLET DE COUR   This represents the final development of the Mascerade, the two running parallel to each other until the time of Louis XIV, at whose death the *genre* faded quickly away. It is difficult to distinguish between the two, but in general it may be said that the Ballet de Cour was part of the Mascerade. It was popular with Henri II, Henri III and Henri IV and Louis XIII; the last-named composed complete Ballets, including the music.

It was danced entirely by the Courtiers, with whom the Royal Family mixed—in the Mascerade the King usually remained an onlooker. The dances grew more and more dignified as time went on—the heels of the dancers' shoes meanwhile growing higher. From the ebullience of the Mascerades of Henri II, the dance styles went out of fashion and, except for the Menuet and Pavane, almost disappeared from view. Finally, the dancing became mere posturing and dignified walking to the strains of the music, the whole being embellished with costumes and décor of supreme magnificence. Spoken dialogue went out altogether, and it ceased for the time to be a dramatic performance. In due course, however, it merged into the Comédie-Ballet, the Opéra-Ballet, and, finally, into Ballet as known to-day.

BOURRÉE   A brisk dance in common or alla breve time, of French origin, commencing on the last crotchet of the incomplete bar. It is usually in flowing quavers.

CHACONNE   There are two varieties:
   1. A dance style in triple time, upon an Ostinato, or constantly repeated melody which may appear in any part and may be inverted or retrogressed.
   The Chaconne appears in orchestral and dramatic music, and is slender in texture and light in idea, unlike its brother the Passacaglia. Some authorities maintain that the Ostinato remains in the bass, but this is not by any means so.

EXAMPLE

Chaconne—*King Arthur* (Purcell)

   2. A brisk movement in triple time in Old Rondo Form. Here the Ostinato principle is transferred to the main material and rests upon its own laurels, thus forming an early species of "Ronde" or Rondo. It was customary to end an Opera with a Chaconne sung and/or danced by the assembled company, this becoming a tradition until Rameau broke away from it. The Chaconne then appeared whenever required. Couperin included some in his several "Ordres", but called them "Passacailles". The character of these is more akin to that of the Chaconne, and they appeared before the two styles became interchanged and the Passacaglia took on a more serious note.

EXAMPLE

Le Bourgeois Gentilhomme (Lully)

COURANTE   There are two varieties, the French and Italian. The French is in quick 3/2 time, the cadences usually altering the rhythm to 6/4. The Italian is in 3/2 or 3/4 time, and is perfectly smooth in even-quaver movement.

DIVERTISSEMENT   An interlude in a ballet programme, during which unconnected solo dances are performed by the stars of the company as a relief to the full ballets. This is expressly intended to attract attention to the dancer in question. It bears some affinity to the Concerto Cadenza; although it is not extemporised, the two intentions are similar. The Divertissement is danced in front of a black backcloth.

GALLIARD A stately Italian dance much in vogue in this country in the time of Queen Elizabeth I. In triple time, its tune was dignified and slow moving, while the underlying harmonies gave it momentum. "God Save the King" is said to have all the elements of a first-rate Galliard. Similar good examples can be found in the carol "Remember, O thou man" and in Purcell's famous Minuet in D, if one can imagine more massive harmonies than those originally written for the piece as a Minuet. The Galliard is often paired with the Pavan.

GAVOTTE A moderately paced dance in alla breve time, commencing on the second half of the bar; the dancers raise their left feet on the third beat. The steps are one to every two beats. It is usually chordal rather than flowing, and is sometimes followed by a Musette.

GIGUE The only dance of English origin, known as the Jig. In the classical Suite it is in contrapuntal style, in compound duple or quadruple time. It is written in the fugato manner, the second section opening with the tune by inversion, often in another voice.

MENUET A stately French dance in triple time, usually beginning on the last beat of the bar. The dancers take one step to each bar. There are often two Menuets in succession, da capo, the second Menuet eventually being known as the Trio.

MUSETTE Literally, "bag-pipes" or "drone". It often follows the Gavotte. Its technical description would be "a piece founded upon a Pedal-Point".

PAS DE DEUX, TROIS, QUATRE, ETC. A dance-movement in a ballet for two, three, four or more dancers.

PASSACAGLIA A dance style in triple time upon an Ostinato which, like that of the Chaconne, may appear in any part and may be inverted or retrogressed. Organ composers adopt it in preference to the Chaconne as being more dignified, although originally the characters of the two dance styles were reversed.

EXAMPLES

Passacaglia and Fugue in C minor (Bach)
Passacaglia—Sonata in E minor (Rheinberger)

PAVAN A stately dance of Italian origin in duple time. It was extremely popular at the Courts of the Valois Kings of France, where it formed the concluding movement of the Fêtes and Ballets de Cour; the entire Court, headed by the King and his Queen (or possibly Lady of the moment), danced out to the supper room in dignified procession to its rhythms. The dignified tune is always backed by an even-quaver (pizzicato) figure, suggestive of the lute.

Modern composers have used the pavan. The French ballet composer Léo Delibes (although hardly "modern") wrote a well-known one in his opera "Le Roi l'a dit", which illustrates the point raised in the preceding paragraph, while Ravel's *Pavane pour une Infante défunte* (Princess, be it noted, not Child) represents the mourning dance round the bier in a Spanish Cathedral. Vaughan Williams has also written a "Pavane of the Heavenly Host" in his *Job*.

The Pavan is usually paired with the Galliard, an example of this pairing also appearing in *Job* ("Galliard of the Sons of the Morning").

SARABANDE A solemn Spanish dance in triple-time, with the accent on the second beat of the bar. It is often followed by one or more Variations, referred to as "Doubles" (French, and pronounced as such and not as in English) or Agréments.

TARANTELLE A brisk Neapolitan Dance in compound duple time similar to the Saltarello. It is mainly in even quavers whose brilliant progress is interrupted from time to time by emphatic rhythmic passages.

INSTRUMENTAL FORMS

BALLADE A composition, usually for the piano, which has an avowed or suggested romantic impulse. It is comparable with the vocal "Ballad" in that it tells some story or other, otherwise it has no connection therewith. The Ballade may be a movement in straightforward ternary form or may be extended to the length of one of the symphonic forms; but there is nothing arbitrary about it. However, there is usually more formal design than in the "Rhapsody", owing to the fundamental literary or pictorial background. Chopin's "Ballades", for example, are works in themselves; those of Brahms are more in the nature of "Pieces".

CADENZA A passage in a Concerto introduced solely for the purpose of displaying the technical prowess of the performer. Originally it was extemporised, the early Concertos of Handel marking the places by a pause and the word "Cadenza". This called for considerable inventive skill, but in due time invention was supplanted by technique. The performer executes a Free Fantasia upon the themes of the movement, passing through whatever keys he likes and signalling his return to the tonic by a prolonged trill upon the leading note over dominant harmony. This indicates the end of the Cadenza.

Schumann and the later romantic composers adopted the custom of composing the cadenzas for themselves, thus relieving the performer of the responsibility of thinking creatively. Many performers, however, wrote and published their own Cadenzas for those classical works which hitherto required improvisation. Not all were successful, as few of these composers had any creative instincts. It is now possible to perform Beethoven's Violin Concerto, for example, with each cadenza written by a different composer.

Most performers like Cadenzas. Some people, however, find them exceedingly wearisome, since the interest is lost in what too often becomes simply a series of gymnastic exercises. Indeed, only too often one wishes the performer would do his practising at home.

CANZONA Originating in Italy in the 16th century, the Canzona was an organ transcription of a polyphonic vocal work. In time it took on its own instrumental character. It was fugal in style, and comprised more than one section—Bach's Canzona in D minor for Organ is in two sections, the first in quadruple, and the second a Variation in triple time, the notes being rhythmically altered and the shape of the theme slightly modified.

The term is also applied to a decorative movement of a baroque nature whose lyrical qualities are rhapsodic and free. In this case the work is a Canzona only by courtesy, so to speak, but the word aptly describes its whole format.

CASSATION A type of Serenade, but applying to one expressly composed for performance at a street corner or outside a particular house, the instrumentation being specially suitable for this purpose. Most of them were scored for wind instruments. The name derives either from the German *Gasse*, meaning "street", or the Spanish *Casa*, meaning "house".

It consisted of dance movements, but there was never any formal exigency about it. In due course the name fell into disuse and that of Serenade took its place. It is, indeed, difficult to distinguish between the two, save that the orchestration of the Cassation would be somewhat thicker and louder than that of the Serenade.

CHAMBER MUSIC Music written for a number of performers small enough to be accommodated in a room, in a style calling for individual proficiency. It has been described as a conversation between instruments. It is not usual to include music for piano alone in this category, although that for a single string or wind instrument appears to find a niche there. In general, therefore, it implies concerted performance by two to nine players; beyond this number a conductor is necessary.

However, to-day the Chamber Orchestra has become fashionable, and the implication of the term has thus adopted a wider aspect. The Chamber Orchestra is differentiated from the ordinary orchestra by containing not more than one player for each instrumental part. A still wider concept of the term has aligned it with the Small Orchestra, and here duplication of string players is usual. The term Chamber Orchestra is thought to be more dignified than Small.

Chamber Music combinations are almost inexhaustible in their permutations. Originally the String or Wind Duo, Trio, or Quartet were the fundamental constituents, these descending from the earlier Sonata da Camera for harpsichord, violin(s) and 'cello. It was not long before string and wind instruments were combined. When the piano took on its own individuality the style became known as Accompanied Chamber Music, although the piano did a great deal more than merely accompany.

Chamber Music has always been regarded as an aristocratic form of music-making, its performance requiring specialised study. Some of the leading String Quartets have resolutely refused to play anywhere and anything save in combination, thus acquiring a standard of ensemble and balance which has often reached perfection. We may mention the Flonzaley, Lener, and Griller Quartets in this respect.

Chamber Music is, of course, the instrumental opposite to the Madrigal, and the Chest of Viols was as much part of the normal furniture of any cultured house as were the Part Books. Its basis, like that of the Madrigal, is polyphony, and development has depended upon its improving technique. The tune, so to speak, is no longer exclusively in the first violin. It demands polyphonic listening; that is why its appeal is limited and its atmosphere slightly rarefied, its passion lying in the grace and charm of interweaving melodic lines.

Although the term Quartet implies a work written for four instruments in symphonic forms consisting of three or four movements, there are many smaller works in the Suite style, the Variation manner, and in the style of short movements or pieces. These earn the description "Quartet", etc., by courtesy.

It would be invidious as well as unnecessary to single out any examples of Chamber Works by the established composers of yesterday and to-day, as the reader has but to glance down a catalogue of miniature scores to find a wealth of material at his command.

CONCERTO This implies in general a work for solo instrument with orchestral accompaniment, but it reached this state only after much development. The term may be traced to the early word "Consort", meaning playing together, which arose from the instrumental Madrigal. It then divided itself into two types, the Concerto da Camera and the Concerto da Chiesa. Like the Sonata da Camera, the former was a series of light dance movements and the latter one of abstract movements suitable for the religious atmosphere of the Church. The following represent the four main styles of Concerto writing:

1. Concerto Grosso (or Concertante)
2. The Solo Concerto
3. The Concerto for a Solo Instrument with Orchestral Accompaniment
4. The Virtuoso Concerto

A return was made later to an elaborate style of Concertante, one prominent instrument playing in the middle of the Orchestra, which filled by no means an accompanimental rôle etc.

1. CONCERTO GROSSO Here all the instruments are of equal importance, but certain instruments often required better performers than others as their music was a shade more difficult. The remainder did not accompany so much as comment and support, antiphonal writing sometimes being a feature when the superior instruments formed themselves into groups. There was no set Form or statutory number of movements.

EXAMPLES

Corelli's Concerto for Christmas Night (eight movements)
Bach's Brandenburg in G (No. 3) (two movements)
Handel's Concerto Grosso in G minor (five movements)

In time, three became the recognised number.

2. SOLO CONCERTO This was a work for a single player whose instrument had two keyboards, the antiphonal effects being obtained by

transference of the hands from one keyboard to the other. They were often coupled, and by playing on the lower one the player could combine all the resources of the instrument. The top keyboard was always less solid than the lower. In the case of the organ the manuals are named Swell and Great, the Great (the lower) has fundamental diapasons of a noble quality.

EXAMPLE

Bach's Italian Concerto

3. CONCERTO FOR SOLO INSTRUMENT WITH ORCHESTRAL ACCOMPANIMENT   This became established with Haydn and Mozart, particularly with the former. The orchestra became subservient to the solo instrument(s) and, except for certain passages known as "tutti", in which the soloist(s) took no part, played a purely accompanimental rôle. The same principle was put forward by Beethoven who, however, made the orchestral parts more significant and important, and in one work, the Piano Concerto No. 4 in G, returned almost to the Concertante style.

4. VIRTUOSO CONCERTO   As interest became centred upon the soloist, so composers placed added emphasis upon brilliance of pianistic technique. Pianists themselves wrote Concertos to suit their own style of playing, Chopin and Liszt being the most notable of their period in this respect.

At that time it was practically impossible to make a reputation only with the solo recital. This may account for the lackadaisical nature of Chopin's orchestral parts, since he knew that rehearsal facilities would be limited and that the audience would be there to hear the piano and not the orchestra. Liszt, however, gave a brilliance to the whole concept which threatened to bring it into some disrepute among musicians, for this very reason. However, he raised the orchestra on to a plane of some importance, and his imitators, like Rubinstein and, to a certain extent, Tchaikowsky, kept it there. Brahms's Piano Concertos, however, while insisting that the soloist be a better performer of his instrument than the orchestral players of theirs, achieved a homogeneity which has never been abandoned. Later examples of this can be found in Rachmaninov's Concertos, which combine opulence with romanticism. At the other end of the scale, there are the well-balanced, if far too slick, Concertos of Saint-Saëns.

It is possible to see how the Concerto-Manner returned to its primitive concertante style by reading the scores of such works as the "Variations Symphoniques" of César Franck, the *Symphonie sur une thème montagnard*,[1] by Vincent d'Indy, the Piano Concerto in G and that in D (for left hand alone) by Maurice Ravel, and the *Sinfonia Concertante* by

---

[1] Described as being "for Orchestra and Piano".

Sir William Walton. The Concerto-Manner has been applied to forms such as Variation and Rhapsody, the works being virtual Concertos written in other than multi-movement forms.

Concertos are written for any number of instruments, either in solo or in combination. The repertoire of the Piano is the largest, since it is the only instrument capable of standing up against the full force of the orchestra. The violin, viola, and 'cello require subtle judgment and skill, and composers do not find themselves so attracted to them. Particularly difficult is the 'Cello Concerto, since the instrument has to be too often in the middle of, or underneath, the orchestra, and can be too rarely above it; hence the question of balance becomes more vital than anywhere else. Composers do not appear to write more than two each for this instrument.

The Concerto is not a Symphony, although it is composed in the Symphonic Forms, with certain variations. The principles of the two styles are completely different. While the intention of the Symphony is to explore the potentialities of themes, that of the Concerto is to explore those of performers. It may be this exigency which has prevented composers from writing Concertos in four movements, since there is ample scope in the usual three. Curiously enough, the composer and publisher, Litolff, who wrote a good deal of now-forgotten music, is remembered by one of four movements only, the Scherzo, which is found in the normal symphonic scheme, but not in that of the Concerto.

In those works which reflect the original Concertante principle with no extra-important instruments, composers use the ordinary Symphonic Forms. The works thus become Sinfoniettas, and the dividing line is often non-existent. Such works may be exemplified by Goossens's Concertino for Double String Orchestra, Stravinsky's Concerto in D, and John Ireland's Concertino Pastorale, both for string orchestra.

The standard designs used for a Concerto are:

First Movement	Modified First-Movement Form
A species of First-Movement Form	Third Movement
Second Movement	Old Rondo Form

I have used the description "A species of First-Movement Form" advisedly because, although conforming in outline with the basic design, it varies certain elements. It is as follows:

Enunciation	*Middle Section*	*Recapitulation*
(Orchestra alone)	Development	
First Subject in tonic key		First Subject in tonic key
Connecting Episode		Connecting Episode

(*Enunciation*)	(*Middle Section*)	(*Recapitulation*)
Second Subject in tonic key		Second Subject in tonic key
Codetta		Cadenza
Repeat of Enunciation with Solo Instrument, the themes being varied and the Second Subject appearing in Dominant or other related key		Coda

Thus the repeat of the Enunciation is essential and not optional, and it varies both in material and key. This is called the Double Enunciation (Exposition). Some regard the First Enunciation as an Introduction, but this is quibbling. The interpolation of the Cadenza will be noted; this is not unique to the First Movement and may appear in any or all.

CONCERTINO A little Concerto whose proportions are smaller and whose material is slighter than those of the Concerto. It holds exactly the same relation to the big style as does the Sonatina to the Sonata and the Sinfonietta to the Symphony.

DIVERSION A fanciful pseudonym for variation having no affiliations with Divertimento or Divertissement. Sir Edward German's "Theme and Six Diversions" may be described as the presentation of a theme in diverse ways.

DIVERTIMENTO Another name for a Serenade, although it is not a work dedicated to any particular person or written for any particular celebration. It consists of a series of dance movements intended purely for entertainment purposes performed as a background for conversation. The older composers were often commissioned to write in this style, and were not ashamed to do so. The instrumentation varies according to the local resources. There is no set form.

DUET A movement or work for two singers or players, often referred to as a Duo. There is usually no accompaniment, although it is not unknown for a piece to be described as a "Duet for Two with piano accompaniment".

Four hands at one piano is the most usual form of Duet, and is only slightly less satisfactory than those at two pianos, since in the former the result sounds like one enormous piano, the whole range of the instrument sounding most of the time. With two instruments the antiphonal effects are always charming, and the climaxes superb. Max Reger, in his *Variations and Fugue on a Theme by Beethoven,* covered almost the entire range of possibilities in this medium.

St. George's, Windsor, has an organ with two consoles, the idea of

Sir Walford Davies. The weakness is that the effect is mainly optical, since the same sets of pipes do duty for both players. From the players' point of view, however, the principle is interesting. The writer on one occasion experienced keen delight over an extemporisation between two players, which was absolutely spontaneous. Those in the nave, down below, however, thought that one player was at work, and thus the interest was proved to have been psychological as well as optical.

ÉTUDE Although this implies a study upon some particular figure of executant technique, it has come to be applied to any piece which does not suggest some more definite title to its composer, the word "Piece" seemingly having something derogatory about it. Composers affect the French word, since the English "Study" is too redolent of interminable athematic finger exercises containing the minimum of musical feeling. The term may, however, apply to a study of some particular theme in which its resources are penetrated to their depth. Consequently, the term *Études Symphoniques*, as composed by Schumann, applies to the permutations of the theme. Each particular Étude in this work, however, bears entirely upon some pianistic device, and is a complete piece in itself.

EXTEMPORISATION The art of playing "without thinking", so to speak, the musical ideas shaping themselves on the spur of the moment. A highly alert state of mind is required, and comparatively few are capable of achieving it, although many wander from key to key under the impression that they are extemporising. The ideal extemporisation should sound like a written-down composition—but a composition should never sound like a written-down extemporisation.

It should be practised in solitude until proficiency is attained, and then used sparingly. A certain elderly organist boasted to the writer that when, as a young man, he was appointed to a certain church, he wrote out literally hundreds of fragmentary themes for extemporisation. He put them all in a hat which hung in the hall, and as he left his house to go to a service, he took one out at random and extemporised his in-going or out-going (according to the nature of the fragment) voluntary on it. Doubtless by the end of the forty-odd years in which he did duty at that long-suffering church he acquired some facility and invention, but one feels sorry for the congregations during the student-period.

On the Continent the church services call for frequent bursts of extemporised interludes, and facility in this is one of the main parts of the organist's equipment. Those who heard them say that César Franck's extemporisations were superlative. To-day people go far to hear Marcel Dupré, the Frenchman, and Hendrik Andriessen, the Dutchman; but one can take any big church almost at random in Paris and be sure of hearing first-class playing of this nature. It can be most inspiring and spiritually uplifting because of its fundamental spontaneity.

FANTASIA This is of two kinds:

1. A movement of a particular type.
2. A movement written upon an already existent theme.

1. Rather more of the bravura type than the Rhapsody, the Instrumental Fantasia is usually splendid in conception and highly decorative in style. It is invariably brilliant and shows off the performer's technique to its greatest advantage. In the style of an extemporisation, it is bound by no formal exigencies and carries out its meaning in its general "fancy". Jean Jacques Rousseau, in his *Dictionnaire de Musique*, maintains that it can never be written down, since, once it has been committed to paper, it ceases to be a Fantasia.[1] There is some justification for this, perhaps, but it does not alter the style of the work. The ideal Fantasia would be an extemporisation that sounds both like a written-down work, and an extemporisation (in spite of the remark on p. 40). J. S. Bach wrote a good example in the Fantasia preceding the Fugue in G minor, whose consistent growth and sustained continuity, while being formless, give the impression of immediate spontaneity. The growth can, however, be perfectly formal and well-balanced, as in Handel's Fantasia in C and Bach's Fantasia in G, the latter falling into two sections, the first bravura and the second strongly harmonic. Mozart's Fantasia in C minor, with the Piano Sonata in C minor, divides itself into four sections, with Coda, is well contrasted in style, and dramatically conceived; there is no thematic cohesion.

2. Composers often take well-known themes and spin them together symphonically, or vary and reorganise one particular tune. Vaughan Williams's *Fantasia on Christmas Carols* and his *Fantasia on Greensleeves* illustrate two different aspects, the former being an interweaving of several tunes, the latter a harmonisation of two tunes, the second a Folk-tune, the whole in ternary form.

At the very lowest degree of the scale there is the pot-pourri of operatic and other airs which is simply a succession of tunes, often banal in character and always written for a technical purpose—in the last century composer-executants wrote *Variations Brillantes* on well-known operatic

---

[1] "Pièce de musique instrumentale qu'on exécute en la composant. Il y a cette différence du *caprice* à la *fantaisie*, que le caprice est un recueil d'idées singulières et disparates que rassemble une imagination échauffée, et qu'on peut même composer à loisir; au lieu que la *fantaisie* peut être une pièce très-régulière, qui ne diffère des autres qu'en ce qu'on l'invente en l'exécutant, et qu'elle n'existe plus si-tôt qu'elle est achevée. Ainsi le caprice est dans l'espèce de l'assortiment des idées, et la *fantaisie* dans leur promptitude à se présenter. Il suit de-là qu'un caprice peut fort bien s'écrire, mais jamais une fantaisie; car si-tôt qu'elle est écrite ou répétée, ce n'est plus une *fantaisie*, c'est une pièce ordinaire" (*Dictionnaire de Musique*, de J. J. Rousseau, Citoyen de Génève).

airs simply to demonstrate their digital dexterity. Sir Henry Wood's *Fantasia on British Sea Songs* is nothing more than a succession of well-known tunes strung together for the set purpose of bringing together a serious-minded audience, this being effected by an accelerated performance, with stamping, of the "Sailor's Horn-Pipe" and the massed singing of "Rule, Britannia". This is perfectly excusable, as it formed a democratic climax at the end of a long season of Promenade Concerts, one of whose characteristics was informality. It was never intended to be taken seriously either by performers or listeners.

GROUND   A theme which recurs over and over again while the music proceeds independently above it. When in the lowest part of the harmony, it is known as Ground Bass. It is also referred to as an Ostinato. This term covers the theme when it is transferred to middle or higher parts.

EXAMPLES

"When I am laid in earth", *Dido and Aeneas* (Purcell)
Ostinato, *St. Paul's Suite* (Holst)

INTRODUCTION   1. A short instrumental passage opening a Symphonic work and proving a complete entity in itself.

2. A short passage introducing the opening lines of a song or instrumental piece.

1. Following on the short rhythmic passage which opened the original Overture, Haydn established the Introduction as an integral part of the Symphony, a practice which was sometimes followed by Mozart, and by Beethoven in seven of his nine Symphonies, and in two of his Piano Sonatas. It served not so much to introduce the themes as to settle the audience before the Symphony or Sonata proper began. It was rarely referred to in any later movement of the work, although Beethoven quoted it during the first movement of the *Sonata Pathétique*. The shortest Introduction on record is that of the Eroica Symphony by Beethoven, which consists of two tonic chords. (Beethoven originally wrote a gigantic cadence.) Composers using the cyclique style use it to lay out the germinals of the material of the whole work.

EXAMPLE

Symphony in B flat (Vincent d'Indy)

2. As the purpose of an Introduction is to introduce something, it is based upon a thematic fragment, usually the opening phrase of the piece which follows. Herein it differs from the Prelude, which is athematic and based upon the accompanimental figure. The ideal Introduction in this case is one which prepares the ear for what follows so that there is no feeling of surprise when the piece begins.

PRELUDE   There are two kinds of Prelude:

1. A short passage opening a vocal or instrumental piece.

2. An independent movement taking its place at the beginning of a Suite, or one standing upon its own feet as a separate entity.

1. This differs from an Introduction in that it anticipates by one or two bars the accompanimental figure of the main theme. It is, therefore, athematic.

2. Consequent upon the above definition, the independent Prelude is a movement based upon some particular figure which may or may not be athematic. When joined to a Suite or any other movement, it maintains its independence and need have no thematic connection with what follows it. This, of course, is the generality, and doubtless there are isolated exceptions. None of Bach's "Forty-Eight" Preludes have any connection with their respective Fugues, and the same applies to the Organ works.

Composers use the term as a title when nothing else suggests itself. Chopin's "Twenty-Four" Preludes are in some cases suggestive of titles —the "Rain-Drop", for example—but they adhere to the fixed figuration principle. The Prelude is naturally not confined to keyboard music, and composers have written Preludes for Orchestra.

EXAMPLES

The Forgotten Rite (John Ireland)
Prelude for Orchestra (Sir John B. McEwen)

PROGRAMME MUSIC   Music which has a literary or pictorial basis. It attempts to relate an event or story, or to paint a landscape in sound. The work can take the form of a single movement (known as a Symphonic Poem) or of a Suite (known as a Symphonic Suite). It is still debatable as to whether music can really fulfil these ends. If it is in the category of realism and translates the sounds or noises of some mechanical instrument, it is usually satisfactory, but it remains to be seen if the result is *music*.

EXAMPLES

The Music of the Machines (Mossolov)
Pacific 231 (Honegger)

In the first instance the sounds of the actual machines are suggested quite convincingly on the musical instruments. In the second, one receives the suggestion of great power and movement; but Honegger in no place sets out to copy the noises of an engine, although they are implied. The two subjects, therefore, are approached quite differently, and Honegger has succeeded in producing a perfectly sound musical expression in a Symphonic Form. The question as to whether music's function is to portray things in this way must be left to individual opinion to decide.

The literary side of music has been exploited since the days of Liszt, and there are a great number of Symphonic Poems in existence. Nevertheless, music cannot in every case portray with any certainty. The progress of Strauss's *Till Eulenspiegel* is easy to follow because of its expressive qualities, and the same may be said of *Don Quixote*; but in the case of *Don Juan* the situation is vague at times, since, although the music is obviously expressing some emotion, it is not possible to associate it with any of the characters unless one is already aware of them. Donna Anna, for example, is represented by one of the loveliest tunes ever written; but it does not tell the listener that it is Donna Anna herself. Don Juan, on the other hand, is more convincing, since his music is expressive of moods and actions. Nevertheless, one could not associate it with Don Juan in person without being previously aware of him. In Tchaikowsky's *Romeo and Juliet* there are obviously love elements and impressions of hasty flights, while the hymn-like chords on wind instruments certainly suggest some kind of ecclesiastical matter; but the protagonists might be anybody. Nevertheless, the work does not really stand upon its own feet without a full explanation of its literary basis. Rimsky-Korsakov's tedious *Scheherazade* in its original form as a Symphonic Poem is descriptive enough; when played as a Symphonic Suite it is convincing and enjoyable, but, except for the obvious storm, it still requires explanatory notes. At the other end of the scale, Saint-Saëns's regrettable *Danse Macabre* certainly suggests dancing skeletons, although it requires the distortion of the *Dies Irae* to confirm it. The clock striking midnight and the cock crowing are sufficiently graphic to give the work a time-setting, but that is not enough. Berlioz's *Symphonie Fantastique* is probably one of the most convincing programme works.

It seems obvious, therefore, that literary music cannot often succeed; but it may be argued that the literary explanation is part of the work itself, which thus becomes two-dimensional. In this case the work succeeds or fails according to whether the listener finds perfect confirmation of the one in the other.

Pictorial Programme Music is easier to achieve, although equally impossible to particularise. Mendelssohn's *Hebrides* Overture is obviously sea music of some kind; but it does not suggest either the Hebrides or Fingal's Cave, or, for that matter, any cave at all. "The Dawn of Day" section in Ravel's *Daphnis et Chloë*—on the other hand, is unmistakable in its associations: this I put to the proof on one occasion when eighteen out of a gathering of twenty, none of whom had ever heard it before, wrote down surprisingly similar and faithful "interpretations" of it. Yet actual daybreak has no actual symphonic sounds about it. Albert Roussel found the happy medium between pictorial romanticism and expressionism in the Aubade from his *Petite Suite*, which begins turbulently and exultantly, and before long introduces obvious bird-songs. Wagner's *Forest Murmurs* is as unmistakable landscape painting as are parts of Beethoven's Pastoral Symphony when the birds sing and the storm rages. However, these are definite musical reproductions of natural phenomena, and are as obvious as the Village Band in the Scherzo of that work. Now and again one finds a compromise which combines the best of the two worlds. Debussy's *Prélude à l'Après-Midi d'un Faune* is a good example of this. Its literary basis upon Mallarmé's poem is indistinguishable, but the situation of the central figure cannot be mistaken. The music does not enlighten the listener as to the Faun's thoughts, but it shows exactly how he is situated. The music gives the impression of a hot sun; the Faun's thoughts and actions are implied, but the actual vision which he sees is non-existent for the listener unaware of the literary basis. The work, therefore, both succeeds and fails. It succeeds in being a beautiful musical landscape, and fails in expressing the purpose of its impulse. It succeeds in its Impressionism, but fails in its more material aspect.

Knowledge of the two bases would appear to be essential for the complete understanding of Programme Music; but complete enjoyment can be, and often is, obtained in blissful ignorance or through an altogether mistaken idea. It can be argued that without complete understanding there can be no complete enjoyment, but the writer confesses to having been deeply moved and thrilled by Strauss's *Don Juan* without having the faintest idea of what it was all about; he was very young at the time.

RHAPSODY Usually spoken of as a wild type of work, completely formless, and in the nature of an extemporisation (an unintentionally cynical reflection). Most Rhapsodies, however, are formally balanced. The term is more a reflection of the spirit of the music than of the technique or form, and the spirit need not necessarily be wild and uncontrolled. The Second Rhapsody for Organ by Herbert Howells is an example of spiritual meditation. Those of Liszt, however, relying, as they do, mainly upon repetition and brilliant technique, have no connection with the spirit, while those of Brahms are well-balanced movements in the symphonic forms. The same may be said of those by Dohnanyi.

Another kind of rhapsodising can be found in objective spiritual exaltation. This is well exemplified in George Butterworth's *A Shropshire Lad*, which is described as *An English Rhapsody*, and bears about it all the signs of the English idiom in its contemplation of an English country scene. The term is as good as any in those situations when invention can devise no other.

ROMANCE   When used to describe a short piece for instruments, it is often of the salon variety, and has some kind of implied romantic impulse. It has no special form and comes within the scope of the piece written for players of moderate ability.

SCHERZO   A light movement which took the place of the Minuet and Trios in Sonatas and Symphonies. It is written in precisely the same form, but, as it is not to be danced, it need not be in triple time. The Scherzo in the Ninth Symphony is in triple, but the Trio is in duple time. There can be more than one Trio, as in Dvořák's Symphony *From the New World*. The Scherzo appears in whole or in part between each Trio; this destroys the ternary symmetry of the movement and gives it the appearance of a Rondo.

Scherzo is also the name given to an individual piece of a light nature, with no reference to a Trio, as in Mendelssohn's Scherzo from his music to *A Midsummer Night's Dream*, and Chopin's Scherzo in B flat minor.

SERENADE   A suite of dance movements composed in honour of some particular person or event. It can be also a single movement played or sung in praise of an individual, the custom being known as serenading. Mozart's *Haffner Serenade* was composed in Salzburg in celebration of the marriage of a friend's daughter.

The instrumentation varies, and some of the older Serenades were written for strings or wind, or both in combination. Like the Cassation, the Serenade was usually played out of doors, but not in the streets (in which case it would have been a Cassation). Mozart's *Eine Kleine Nacht-musik* is probably the best known Serenade in existence; it is for strings only.

Composers have always used the description in place of the more prosaic Suite, since it carries an imaginative and romantic flavour. The style has never been discarded, and lately the habit of evening concerts out of doors has been revived at Hampton Court, at Canterbury, and at other places. Indoor Serenades have also become fashionable, and the whole revival is extremely charming because of its informality. There is a certain difference between the actual Serenade *per se* and the suite so-designated. The former is always much lighter in style and texture than the latter. Brahms's two Serenades are more akin to suites for this reason, as is that by Dvořák. Tchaikowsky's famous *Serenade for Strings* combines the best of two worlds, the Romance and Waltz being pure Serenade music, the "Pièce en forme d'Ouverture" and final "Danse Russe" coming into the category of Suite. Probably a model may be found in Elgar's *Serenade for Strings*, which is basically charming music, intended for pure delight. Of the numerous single-movement so-called Serenades, Glazounow's *Sérénade espagnole* for 'cello and orchestra and that in Delius's music to *Hassan* are among the most familiar, the latter, a gay tune, being sung to "la" with harp (quasi-lute) accompaniment. The German term for the style is *Nachtmusik*, and Gustav Mahler included two movements of this type in his Seventh Symphony.

SERENATA   The Italian style of Serenade differs from the German, for it includes a March, a Minuet, a Scherzetto, and a Canzonetta. In some cases there are two Marches, one at each end. It is usually scored for wind instruments, and bears a distinct relationship to the Cassation, as its performance was not confined to gardens and parks, like the Serenade or *Nachtmusik*. Alfredo Casella wrote a remarkable little *Serenata* for wind instruments which, while fulfilling all the traditional requirements, is written in a truly 20th-century style.

SINFONIA   The name given to the early Overtures, to Cantatas and to the embryo Symphonies by the immediate post-Bach composers. It suggests something dignified and pompous and is fully suitable to the early form of these works.

It is used by composers usually in conjunction with the word "concertante"—Mozart wrote a *Sinfonia Concertante* for violin, viola, and orchestra—and the term implies a "playing together" of music written on symphonic principles, one or more instruments being of prior importance. It is not in any way similar to the Concerto, but may be aligned with the Concerto Grosso. Sir William Walton's *Sinfonia Concertante* for piano and orchestra is a fine example. Although in this work the Piano is the senior instrument in the ensemble, there is nothing perfunctory or accompanimental about the orchestral parts.

SONATA   A work for one or two instruments in at least three and often four movements, each movement being based upon one of the Symphonic Forms. The word implies "Sound" for one or two instruments of any kind. It originated in Italy, where there were two versions:

1. Sonata da Chiesa
2. Sonata da Camera

literally meaning "Sound" for Church, and "Sound" for a room. The Sonata was originally written for string instruments, with continuo.

1. SONATA DA CHIESA   This music was severe and dignified in quality, as befitted its surroundings. It consisted of three movements—a slow introduction leading straight into a quick and often fugato movement; a slow movement, often merely a modulatory episode in the style of an accompanied recitative (but more strictly measured), followed by a quick finale. This formed the basis of the Sonata-proper of the classical German and Austrian composers.

2. SONATA DA CAMERA   Here dignity was thrown to the winds, and

the music was in the style of gay and blithesome dance movements. It conformed more with the Suite than with its brother of the Church and, with the exception of the Menuet, bears little, if any, relationship to the modern Sonata. The stages of its development can be summarised thus:

(a) Monothematic (Binary Form, pre-Haydn)
(b) Bi-thematic (C. P. E. Bach, Haydn, Mozart)
(c) Beethoven
(d) Post-Beethoven (Romantic)
(e) Cyclique

(a) *Monothematic* Scarlatti shaped it into one movement in some kind of dance-style. It was organised upon a succession of modulations through closely-related keys, the theme being treated sequentially, repetitively, and fragmentarily.

(b) *Bi-thematic* C. P. E. Bach widened it by not only introducing a second theme, but by repeating the first section after the second, thus establishing it in ternary form.

(c) *Beethoven* He established the symphonic forms in each movement, widening the existing concept as far as it would go, finally discarding the entire framework. He established the four-movement principle, although later returning to three. The Menuet he replaced by the Scherzo. Further, he made the entire work thematic by basing the Bridge Passages (Connecting Episodes) upon elements of the opening theme instead of leaving them as mere modulatory flourishes. He widened the principles of key-relationship by taking the music further afield, and was not particular as to the key of his Second Subject (see Waldstein Sonata). The original idea of a "Subject" was changed into that of a "Theme Group", and the Second Subject contained a number of themes (or consisted of a number of "parts"), and in most cases was far wider in scope and resource than the first.

(d) *Post-Beethoven (Romantic)* Beethoven's immediate successors used the Sonata to express avowed romantic feelings and pictures, moving it away from the strictly classical outlook. They widened the original scheme mainly as regards tonality, leaving the framework as they received it from Beethoven. It was not experimented with until much later.

(e) *Cyclique* This consists of binding the movements together thematically by means of rhythmic alterations or actual quotations, in full, of the material of the first movement, thus giving the Sonata unification. Beethoven had already done this in a small way. The idea was firmly established by César Franck and Liszt, and imitated by Saint-Saëns. Vincent d'Indy made it a living and significant principle, and others followed him. The metamorphosis of themes which ensued often passes unrecognised until the music is read analytically, and when this is the case, the process may be said to be completely successful. The principle eventually led to the one-movement Sonata, written either as one continuous whole, but often resulting simply in a single first movement; or a succession of linked movements, each section leading into the next.

There is nothing arbitrary about the form or design of a Sonata. Composers choose their Forms to suit their ideas. "It is the material which decides the form, not the form the material"—a dictum of Vincent d'Indy which contradicts those who maintain that composers pour their ideas into "moulds". Possible forms for each movement are:

First Movement: First Movement (or Sonata) Form, with or without Introduction.

Second Movement: Modified First-Movement (or Sonata) Form, or an Air and Variations.

Third Movement: Menuet and Trio, or Scherzo and Trio.

Fourth Movement: Sonata-Rondo Form, or Old Rondo Form, or First Movement (or Sonata) Form.

As has been said, nothing definite can be laid down, and it is easy to find examples, particularly of first and second movements, which do not conform with the above suggestions; but in general the above is the custom.

For some reason or other, it is not customary to refer to a work for three or more instruments as a "Sonata", although it may be written in the same Symphonic Forms. In these cases, the work is referred to by the number of instruments concerned—Trio, Quartet, Quintet, Sextet, Septet, Octet, and Nonet—yet the works are virtually Sonatas.

SONATINA A little Sonata, a description justified because the material is slighter, the texture more slender, and the formal exigencies shorter than the full-size Sonata. Formal balance is maintained all through, and the symphonic forms it uses are in no way different save in length.

The Sonatas of Beethoven's contemporaries, particularly Hummel and Dussek, although called Sonatas, are in reality Sonatinas, since they do not compare in scope with the thirty-two Piano Sonatas of Beethoven. Beethoven himself wrote Sonatinas (op. 49, Nos. 1 and 2) which find their places in the canon. Sonatinas are supposed to be good introductions to Sonatas when small hands and too youthful technique cannot rise to the greater heights. Nowadays they frequently require as good a technique as Sonatas; but the underlying all-round diminution remains the same as ever it was.

SUITE Known originally in France as an Ordre, in Germany as a Partita, in England as a Lesson, and in Italy as a Sonata da Camera, it consists of a number of pieces which may or may not have thematic connection. From the 16th century onwards the Suite consisted of a succession of Dance movements together with a Prelude which, in turn, was called Sinfonie, Préambule, or Overture. There were four basic movements, and others could be added between the third and fourth. Many of the original dances have long since passed into oblivion and remain as charming names only—Magot, Branle, Volte, etc.

The Suite was opened with a Prelude or an Allemande; often there were both. There were sometimes two Menuets, da capo, and Doubles (Variations) to the Sarabande. These Doubles applied to other dances as well. While the style of the dances was maintained, with some composers they were not actually danceable, the connection being held through rhythmic characteristics. The Suite gradually merged into the Serenade, Divertimento, and Cassation, but as a series of Dance styles it fell into oblivion. Its revival took the form of independent movements of all kinds, and any series of pieces under one cover and one title came to constitute a Suite. As a significant force in musical designs it has had its day, but it is a useful means of gathering together separate movements from a large-scale work like a Ballet or Opera, thus preserving them for concert use.

Sometimes a Suite carries a Programme, in which case it is known as a Symphonic Suite, although there may not be any considerable symphonic development in the movements. Suites constitute useful items in programmes where Sonatas would be too long and isolated short pieces too disjointed.

SYMPHONY   Literally "sound for orchestra"—it would be wrong according to our notions of nomenclature to describe it as a "Sonata for Orchestra", although its constituent elements are exactly similar to those of the Sonata. (The French composer Alkan wrote what he called a Symphony for Piano, but nobody else has thought it worth while to disturb the placid waters of tradition and, indeed, it seems pointless to do so in this respect, although it might draw attention to an individual work which otherwise might be submerged in the welter of Sonatas of all kinds.) The resources of the orchestra naturally offer more varied and manifold opportunities to the composer than do the one or two instruments of the Sonata, and in the majority of cases the elaborate Symphony is always longer than the elaborate Sonata.

The Symphony is a development from the Overture of the pre-Haydn composers. Its emergence from the chrysalis stage was effected by three composers working simultaneously in different countries. Although the formulation of the Symphony as known to-day is generally credited to Haydn, it was not created by him, or by Boccherini or Gossec. Until quite late in Haydn's lifetime the Symphony was just an Overture and was known as such, its purpose being entertainment and nothing else.

The historical development may be summarised:

(*a*) Primitive (Sammartini).
(*b*) Bi-thematic Classicism (Haydn, Boccherini, Gossec, Mozart).
(*c*) Beethoven.
(*d*) Post-Beethoven (Romantic)
(*e*) Cyclique.

In general, what has been said about the Sonata applies equally well to the Symphony, with the exception that it has remained in four movements. The inclusion of the Menuet may have been dictated by the wish to relieve concentrated listening with a well-known dance style, whose rhythm immediately cleared the atmosphere of whatever subjective feelings the second movement may have conjured up, and prepared the ear for the new music of the Finale.

The use of names became general after Beethoven, and the purely classical approach remained in abeyance until Brahms, when it made a reappearance. To-day composers have returned to it, and the majority of new Symphonies by young composers heard nowadays suggest that they are nearly all passing through a phase of extreme neurosis.

The Symphony has been regarded as marking a landmark in a composer's creative output. The older musicians waited until they were sure of their technique before attempting it, and thus put into it their deepest and most personal thoughts, serious and gay, the thoughts being born of human experience. To-day, too many young composers open their careers with a Symphony, this usually leading post-haste to a second, and to a third. The promise sometimes shown by the first is not always sustained because enthusiasm and ambition blind their composers to what the more experienced mind realises to be absolutely necessary—namely, that the creative impulse requires to be refuelled even when it is mature, and that sustained continuity and development cannot be maintained without a breathing-space. Mendelssohn tore up twelve Symphonies before displaying his No. 1. This is, perhaps, rather too stringent in view of present-day technique; but it would be encouraging if young composers tore up their second and even third efforts, and, when stranded with nothing to say, would refrain from talking, for the Symphony offers too many opportunities for empty rhetoric under the guise of "noble thoughts".

SYMPHONIETTA more often SINFONIETTA This holds exactly the same position in relation to the Symphony as does the Sonatina to the Sonata, with the additional quality of lighter orchestration and a smaller orchestral requirement.

SYMPHONIC POEM A work usually in First-Movement Form with a literary or pictorial basis (see Programme Music).

TOCCATA   A piece to be "touched" on the keyboard,[1] the opposite of Cantata (to be sung). Toccatas are of a brittle character designed to show off the percussive powers of the instrument and the digital dexterity of the player. Conceived on the bravura pattern, the movement amply illustrates its name. Among famous Toccatas may be mentioned those in D minor and F for the organ by J. S. Bach, that in D minor for the clavichord by Purcell, and that in the Fifth Organ Symphony by Widor. There is no set form and the movement resembles a loose kind of extemporisation, often including unmeasured cadenzas. Debussy and Ravel have written Toccatas representative of modern pianistic technique.

VOLUNTARY   The organ piece or work played before or after a service of any kind. The organist is free not only to choose the music of the Voluntary, but also to decide whether to include it or not, there being no controlling rubric or liturgical place for it. Organ Voluntaries are usually of a quiet nature before the service and loud after it. The Voluntary before the service sets the mood for worship. The dynamics do not matter as much as the quality and quantity of the music chosen. Much that is suitable for an organ recital is out of place as a Voluntary, since anything meretricious or virtuosic attracts the attention of the faithful to the prowess of the performer. Similarly, the typical organ Voluntary sounds tame in an organ recital, and organists usually draw a distinct dividing line between the two.

A curious tradition has evolved whereby anything called a Fugue, particularly if its composer's name is Bach, is suitable as a Voluntary. This remarkable theory is derived entirely from the fact that Fugue has been regarded as an extremely learned texture and, therefore, anything which comes from the brain must be devotional. This takes no account of Bach's Scherzo Fugues, such as that in A minor with its preceding athematic Prelude, and that in the Toccata in C major, to say nothing of the Fantasia preceeding the well-known Fugue in G minor, which provides Voluntary music *par excellence*. The writer once heard a congregation dismissed during Lent to Bach's Fugue alla Gigue.

Thomas Tans'ur's *New Musical Dictionary* (1766) throws some light upon the subject and we beg leave to quote from it, especially as the writer came across an instance of what Tans'ur says:

"*Voluntary*. A grand Extempore Piece of Musick, performed on the ORGAN before the *Composition* begins etc. In *Divine Service*, it is performed just before the *First Lesson*; which is (or ought to be) *solemn, grand*, and *noble* withal; free from all antick or lascivious Airs, which only corrupt the Mind with impure Thoughts etc. This, I say, should be such *Harmony* as may expel from our Souls all *Gloom* and *Sadness*,

---

[1] Monteverdi called the orchestral opening to his *Orfeo* a Toccata.

so as to raise and *prepare* us for Admission of those *sacred Truths* which are to follow in the *Lessons* of the *Old* and *New Testament*. It should call in our *Spirits*, delight our *Ears*, and recreate our *Minds*; and so fill our Souls with pure and *heavenly Thoughts*, that nothing may remain in us but *Peace* and *Tranquility*. It should diffuse a *Calmness* all round us, and, as much as possible, give us such a *Taste of Heaven*, here on Earth, as to make us ambitious of the *full Fruition* thereof, after we depart this troublseome (*sic*) Life, etc., etc. which may God in His Infinite *Mercy* grant."

This would come immediately after the Psalms.[1]

In the time of Handel, Voluntary-playing reached a very high standard, and certain organists, including Handel, would go to hear the blind John Stanley at St. Alban's, Holborn, play the concluding Voluntary. This was the forerunner of the modern organ recital.

---

[1] In 1917 the writer did duty as organist at a London church where it was the custom to extemporise a few bars after the Psalms. Nobody knew whence it derived or how it had crept into the customs of the particular church, which was not in any way ritualistic or enterprising. The writer can only hope that he fulfilled some of Thomas Tans'ur's requirements.

DRAMATIC FORMS

COMÉDIE-BALLET This is a stage play with incidental music, including dancing coincidental with the action. It originated in the great collaboration between Molière and Lully, the most famous work being *Le Bourgeois Gentilhomme*. In certain cases the scope of the entire work became very nearly operatic, and the book of *Psyché*, admirable as a stage play, has also all the elements of an Opera-Libretto. The Comédie-Ballet gave place to the Opéra-Ballet after the split between Lully and Molière, and the latter's death.

On occasions the Ballet and the Dialogue were kept apart, the former being used as "Intermèdes" to afford relief from the latter. The connection can be seen here with the Ballet section in Opera. In the case of the Intermède, however, it made no difference to the description of the work as a whole, since it was of sufficient substance to become an integral part of the Comédie.

ENTR'ACTE This is an orchestral movement played between the acts of an Opera, with the curtain lowered. Its intention is either to fill up the gap between the acts and so maintain some kind of musical continuity (drowning conversation, if possible), or to set the mood for what is to follow. It may also denote the passage of time, as in Mascagni's *Cavalleria Rusticana*.

The term also applies to stage plays with or without incidental music, in the latter case the intention being simply to supply a musical background to movement, conversation, and tea-drinking. It is rarely listened to, and the applause which follows, sometimes unexpectedly, is an acknowledgment of an awareness of something which has passed unnoticed until its cessation. Another term is "Intermezzo", which is used more generally than the French "Entr'Acte".

INCIDENTAL MUSIC This is of two kinds:

1. That correlated with the stage action.
2. That intended to set moods and to heighten situations.

1. As has been said, the ideal is to be found in the Comédies-Ballets of Molière and Lully, and dramatists have always found a place for music. Shakespeare's plays abound with it.

The score may consist simply of one or more songs or instrumental pieces performed on the stage. In many cases the actors mime the playing of the instrument, the actual instrument being played either in the wings or in the orchestral pit. This sometimes has its amusing aspects.

The heydays of incidental music in England would appear to have been those of Henry Purcell, and of Sir Henry Irving and Sir Edward German, whose Shakespearean and other period productions were lavish, colourful, and distinctly individual. Among the many fine scores composed for this purpose Gabriel Fauré's for *Shylock*, and Delius's for Flecker's *Hassan* should be mentioned.

The days of the full symphonic orchestra are over where the theatre is concerned, and composers have to fit their ideas to suit a limited budget—this means composing for the smallest possible number of instruments.

2. This kind is familiar through its association with films, radio, and television, although the last named approaches the theatre too closely to require much of it.

Film music is the most extravagantly paid of all types of musical work, and it is also the most laborious, since it has to be devised and timed to the split second. The lavish American "musical", with its score written in the true Hollywood manner, is always colourful, and those who do not take their film-drama seriously find it a happy means of relaxation. The dividing-line between the music which is part of the action and that which heightens situations is clearly drawn, and although human tragedies do not take place as a rule to the accompaniment of a full symphony orchestra, the psychological side of the situation asks for this support. The composer has to read the mind of the character and actually to "live" the situation concerned.

Music is more essential for the radio than for the film, since the imagination of the listener is here perpetually in full play. Present-day listening technique has reached such a high standard that voice and music have become completely reconciled, and the one no longer stands in the way of the other. There are many radio plays which do not demand music but get it; there are not many which demand it and do not get it. The composer is not influenced by the need for split-second timing, as he is in film music, and the music can usually be faded in and out to suit the requirements. The score which cuts off its music too suddenly becomes intensely irritating after a while. As in the case of film music, the radio score should be completely "apt" for the script in question. Alas, this is not always the case.

INTERMÈDE This is a French term which finds no counterpart elsewhere. It usually applies to the dancing section which the early operatic composers inserted between the acts of a stage play in order to break the monotony of the spoken dialogue. It was cultivated by Molière and Lully, who used it extensively for this purpose, thus originating the Comédie-Ballet. It hardly had the same significance as the Entr'Acte, since it came more often and was performed with the curtain raised. There was no necessity for there to be any connection with the work in progress, and sometimes the Intermèdes were plays within plays—that is to say, one followed another in alternation, so that by separating the play from the Intermèdes, each could form a

perfectly satisfactory entity on its own. It may be said to have been
a necessitous innovation, since Lully's Académie Royale de Musique
consisted of a complete opera and ballet company; previous to this,
Intermèdes were introduced to satisfy the wishes of the courtiers of the
Valois Kings of France—who not only danced, but enjoyed watching
others do it.

MASCERADE This is a form of Court entertainment popular in
France in the time of the Valois. It was imported in its most splendid
form from Italy by Catherine de Medici. It consisted of a miscellaneous
sequence of events, including dancing, poetic recitations, processions,
and tournaments. The best poets available collaborated in the books,
the most notable being Ronsard. The whole affair was a mythological
and symbolical eulogy of the reigning sovereign, one of the foremost
features being the issue of *cartels* (or challenges) to whomsoever would
question the supremacy of the King in every field.

Another type was the Mascerade nautique, which consisted of processions of mechanically propelled sea-monsters. These entertainments
in general were known as Fêtes de Cour. They remained fashionable
until Henry IV instigated the Ballet de Cour.

The word is also used in connection with the Masked Ball, a different
type of entertainment, referring to the masks worn by the ballroom
dancers, but, as the possibility of fancy dress costume is not ruled out,
the dancers can be said to be masquerading as someone else.

MASQUE A stage work consisting of songs, dances, and spoken dialogue resembling the French Mascerade and Fête de Cour. It is unlike
the Mystère, which also combines the three elements, as it does not
necessarily have a religious bias. It is an essentially English species of
dramatic work, and originated in the 16th and 17th centuries, Blow
and Purcell being the most prominent exponents in the latter period.
A later example can be found in the *Masque of King Alfred*, by Thomas
Augustus Arne, remembered solely for "Rule, Britannia", while Vaughan
Williams described his *Job* as "A Masque for Dancing". The subjects
were always symbolical. It could have paved the way to the formation
of English Opera, but did not do so.

MYSTÈRE A dramatised version of a Biblical story, performed with
spoken dialogue, music, and dancing, originating in Italy and passing
to France, where it took root. Performances date from the Medieval
ages, when they were given in churches. In due time they moved to
the church porch and thence to the market-places and town squares,
where the laity took them over from the clergy. Although the sacred
basis was maintained, and although there was a certain amount of
profanity in the sacred plays, once they reached the open air, they
became more profane than sacred.

The populace formed the chorus, and the cast often ran into hundreds. Much was extemporised, and in the earliest stages resembled what is known to-day as a "charade". The performances lasted for days on end and were produced with as much splendour as local resources could provide. Much of the music was liturgical, but there was also some specially composed; the music was always sung in unison.

The style, like that of the Opéra-Ballet, is going through a period of revival, since it offers great possibilities for a combination of all the arts. Modern examples may be found in Honegger's *Jeanne d'Arc au Bucher* and Claude Delvincourt's *Lucifer*. If not actually Biblical nowadays, the works always have a religious bias.

OPERA This is a musical version of a stage play in which singing takes the place of speech. This generality must be immediately qualified in consideration of the various categories into which the *genre* falls, for opera with spoken dialogue is still opera—of a particular kind. The categories are:

1. Opera
2. Opéra-Comique
3. Opéra-Bouffe
4. Operetta
5. Opéra-Ballet

1. OPERA Originating in Italy, opera in its truest and purest style was imported to France by Cardinal Mazarin, and in due course the genuine French style emerged at the hands of a Florentine, Jean Baptiste Lully, to become finally established by Jean Philippe Rameau. Its arrival in England was immediately due to the influence of Charles II, who had experienced it at the French Court.[1] The first result of this was *Venus and Adonis*, by Dr. John Blow, a short work hardly warranting the designation of Opera. This was followed by Purcell's *Dido and Aeneas*. *The Siege of Rhodes*, by Davenant and several composers, is often described as the first English Opera, but its layout does not justify this title any more than the *Ballet Comyque de la Royne* of Beaujoyeux justifies its being considered the first real French Opera.

Opera can consist of a string of arias and ensemble numbers, held together by recitatives which cover the conversational sections. With the introduction of recitativo stromentato, the musical web began to tighten until the symphonic concept took hold of composers, and operas became self-contained musical entities, the conversational passages being carried along with sheer music. From this developed the French term "lyrique", and operas became known as "lyriques" because they were sung to measured music throughout.

Meantime the Italian School cultivated the virtuoso style of Opera which grew into Grand Opera, the emphasis being placed on the singer

---

[1] Compare the section on Verse Anthem.

rather than on the music. The orchestral parts were often perfunctory to a degree, and merely added supporting harmonies. The singer indulged in acrobatic cadenzas and florid passages which showed off technical prowess and placed a minimum of importance on the music itself. The coloratura soprano had her heyday in this operatic style, which reached its zenith with Rossini, Bellini, and Donizetti. Nowadays these vocal gymnastics have their humorous aspect to those who rate the musical composition higher than the vocal organ.

2. OPÉRA-COMIQUE   In its broadest terms this implies an opera divided into set arias and ensemble numbers, with conversational passages in spoken dialogue. It was essential that there be a "happy ending". This style took the place of the elaborate mythological opera and had simplicity as its keynote, the audience wanting only easy tunes. In due course the term became applicable to any opera with spoken dialogue, this reaching an absurd point when it could include a work like *Carmen* in its original state. Later, when Debussy's *Pelléas et Mélisande* was produced at the Opéra-Comique, the situation became absurd and Opéra and Opéra-Comique merged into the generic Opéra.

Nowadays the quantity of the work has prior claim over the quality, and any opera which is not tragic and is not composed on the grand scale finds its home in Opéra-Comique. Charpentier's *Louise*, although sung throughout, is definitely Opéra-Comique for both its subject and its lyrical quantities. It would be correct to consider *Die Meistersinger* under the same heading, although its substance is too solid. In Germany the equivalent of Opéra-Comique would be Singspiel, and in England Gilbert and Sullivan.

3. OPÉRA-BOUFFE   This includes parody and absurdity. It is summed up in one name—Offenbach, but not in terms of *The Tales of Hoffman*, which is Opera seria. *La Belle Hélène* and *Orpheus in the Underworld* are good examples.[1]

4. OPERETTA   This is a picturesque work of a light and happy character, of no great musical or literary substance. The libretto usually deals with some pleasing romantic subject, the lovers concerned going through certain difficulties which ultimately resolve themselves to the satisfaction of all concerned, except, perhaps, the villain of the piece, who is usually rendered harmless. The operettas of Reynaldo Hahn and André Messager in France and of Franz Lehar and Oscar Strauss in Vienna afford characteristic examples of two approaches. In England the applicable term is usually Musical Comedy, and is exemplified in the works of Lionel Monckton, Howard Talbot, and Paul Rubens. The term does not apply on the Continent, where a Comédie-Musicale implies an opera based upon a comedy, often musical throughout. The style has almost died out in England, and there are no more Gaiety

[1] The latter was honoured by a parody, *Orpheus in the Underground*, thus making a parody of a parody.

Girls or Gaiety productions to delight the eye and feast the ear of those seeking pure entertainment. The American version is more elaborate and lavish, and works like *Oklahoma* and *Carrousel* are a species apart. An attempt was made to echo the Musical Comedy in such works as *The Desert Song* and *The Vagabond King*, but these became known as Musical Plays, the term eventually degenerating into the objectionable American abbreviation—Musical, which has its film counterpart.

5. OPÉRA-BALLET This is an essentially French style. Originated by Lully, it was established by Rameau. It then fell into partial disuse, to be revived in the present century by Albert Roussel and other composers. It is a work which has moments of ballet, each related to the subject in some way. It offers excellent opportunities for spectacular production and affords a constant change from vocal music to mime. The style led to the inclusion of a complete Ballet halfway through the Opera which had the attraction of drawing ballet-lovers into the theatre for that moment. It does not seem to have mattered overmuch whether the Ballet had any connection with the Opera or not, and the actual composers of the Opera in question did not always compose the music for the Ballet. In a work like Gounod's *Faust* the Ballet depicts some of the world's great lovers and courtesans, danced to the most innocuous of tunes. The connection between these and Marguerite's downfall is obvious if far-fetched. The failure of Wagner's *Tannhäuser* in Paris was due entirely to the fact that what dancing there was came at the beginning of the work and not in the usual place. The Jockey Club, whose members were interested in legs rather than larynxes, considered that they had been slighted, and behaved accordingly. The style was revived in Roussel's *Padmâvatî*, which combined the early Opéra-Ballet tradition and requisites with the finest 20th-century thought.

An Opera that happens to have incidental dancing is not an Opéra-Ballet, for the dancing must be an integral part of the whole work. The fact that the Priestesses disport themselves, and that the Public indulges in a so-called "Bacchanale", does not mean that Saint-Saëns's *Samson et Délila* can be classed as an Opéra-Ballet any more than the ballet in Goossens's *Judith* makes that work anything but an Opera.

PASTORALE The name given to an early type of Opera which combined singing and dancing. It developed in France in the pre-Lully days, and the *Pastorale d'Issy* (so-called from the place of its production) is one of the first titular instances of it—the word had already been used generically. Robert Cambert, the immediate predecessor of Lully, wrote a notable one, and Molière's *Pastorale Comique* (the word "comique" having humorous affiliations) was set to music by Lully. As it suggests, it had a rustic setting in which mythological characters mixed with humans, although in the Molière example the "mythological" were the proverbial shepherd and shepherdess. The mediaeval *Jeu de Robin et Marion* was a typical Pastorale. The basic stories were slender; they usually hinged upon the rustic love of two allegedly innocent people and an attack upon the girl's virtue by a sophisticated knight or "superior person". Need it be said that virtue always triumphed?

VOCAL FORMS

AIR   This is the name given to the melodic line of a song, particularly when it is of a cantabile or lyrical quality. It is a more specialised word than "tune" although containing the same implications. Composers use it in default of a characteristic title for both vocal and instrumental music.

ARIA   This is an Air presented under a definite style and form. The Aria is to be found in Operas and Oratorios. Dr. Percy Scholes[1] gives a list of no less than fifteen types. The most common is that known as the "da capo Aria"; this forms a complete ternary structure, the first section ending on the tonic and the second on the dominant, the whole being preceded by an instrumental Introduction based upon the opening bars of the Aria; this Introduction is omitted at the reprise. The Aria flourished in Italian Opera until the end of the 18th century, and a great number of oratorio composers used it.

EXAMPLES

"Have mercy upon me, O Lord" (Bach)   "With verdure clad" (Haydn)
"Rejoice greatly" (Handel)   "Voi che sapete" (Mozart)

Rameau used a style in three sections which does not conform to the ABA principle, since it has completely new music for its third section, thus making it ABC. Although contrast takes the place of unity, the balance is not affected. The first section veers towards the dominant key, the second carefully avoids the tonic key in order to move to the relative major or minor, section C bringing the music back to the tonic; on occasions A modulates to the relative key and B to the dominant.

ARIETTA   As the name suggests, this is a diminutive Aria in which the middle section is omitted; but Simple Ternary Form is not altogether precluded as long as the movement itself is short and to the point.

ARIOSO   This is more measured than the recitativo stromentato; it is more expressive than formal. The term is used rather loosely and often applies to Arietta, but quite erroneously so. The style is not quite so declamatory as is recitativo stromentato, but the general layout is less developed than Aria.

BALLAD   In its purest sense a ballad is a song, probably written on the spur of the moment, commemorating some event. Ballads were

---

[1] *The Oxford Companion to Music* (O.U.P.).

originally sold in the streets in the form of broadsheets. The tunes were simple and the words were not always of a high literary standard. In a good many cases some kind of tune was improvised to fit the metre of the words; consequently it was not impossible for one ballad to have different melodies in different parts of the country. The term, therefore, is more applicable to the verses than to the music. However, during the Victorian era there evolved a species of drawing-room song which became known as a Ballad. This was usually sentimental and was devised solely for amateur music-makers of modest, if not indeterminate, abilities. It became very much the rage and in due course Ballad concerts were given in London for the sole (though undisclosed) purpose of publicising the latest songs. Singers were paid fees to sing new Ballads, since the amateur world would always follow suit. These became known as "Royalty Ballads"; nowadays the principle is referred to by the less generous term, "plugging". The fashion died during the early part of the 1914 War, and as yet has not been revived. Among the foremost composers of Drawing-room Ballads may be mentioned Wilfrid Sanderson, Samuel Liddle, and Florence Aylward, with Fred Weatherley as an indefatigable writer of ballad lyrics.

In the extended form of the Secular Cantata the text is often that of a literary Ballad, as "Lord Ullin's Daughter", and "The Lay of the Ancient Mariner"; but here the term is strictly literary.

CANTATA (SECULAR) Unlike its sacred counterpart, a Secular Cantata can be of any length. The Secular Cantata usually tells some protracted story for chorus and orchestra, with or without soloists. This may be continuous or may be split up into sections. All personal statements are given to a soloist of the sex of the character concerned, and very often the soloist(s) unite(s) with the chorus to obtain a musical effect. An example of this can be found in Coleridge-Taylor's *A Tale of Old Japan*, where the three soloists join the chorus in such a passage as "Lying on the golden sand, Kimi watched his wings expand".

The text for a Secular Cantata can resemble an opera libretto, without action, but as a rule it is that of a long poem or ballad. Omission is usually impossible, as this would destroy the continuity of the verses. The scope of the Secular Cantata can be envisaged from the following:

EXAMPLES

Scenes from the *Saga of King Olaf* (Elgar)

"The Revenge" (Stanford)

"The Mystic Trumpeter" (Harty)

"The Bells" (Holbrooke)

"Sea-Wanderers" (Bantock)

"In Honour of the City" (Walton)

"The Canterbury Pilgrims" (Dyson)

"Hey Nonny No" (Smyth)

A new use and form for the Secular Cantata was suggested by Arnold Schoenberg in his *Ode to Napoleon* for orator and orchestra, which is more than an extended melodrama, in the true sense of the term. It is possible that a future may lie in this style, especially now that ears have become attuned to assimilating speech and music simultaneously through the medium of so many radio plays.

GLEE A term rather loosely applied to a form of vocal ensemble music, tracing its descent from the Madrigal, without the latter's exigencies. It was prominent in the 18th century, but vanished in the first half of the 19th. In its purest form it may be described as a song for male solo voices only, but there are numerous examples for mixed voices which would seem to come into the category. The insistence upon male voices is confirmed by the great number of Glee clubs which flourished in the country during the Glee's popularity. These, again, traced their ancestry from the Madrigalian customs of the 16th century. If one may judge from the contemporary prints of Hogarth and others, the members of the Club sat round a table in an Ale- or Coffee-House and sang Glee after Glee at sight, assisted by copious draughts of punch or coffee, the meetings stretching far into the night. It was probably as innocent a pleasure as any at the time, especially as women were excluded. A happy result of the fashion can be seen in the large quantity of well-written Glees, set to words of a high standard, which were composed for specific clubs by many composers, famous and unknown. Unlike the Madrigal, the Glee started its life as a purely *English* pastime.

MADRIGAL The secular equivalent of the Motet. It originated in Italy, and soon found its way across Europe. The English Madrigal of the 16th century still reigns supreme. It started as a kind of domestic music-making; part-singing at sight was then regarded as a distinguishing mark of a good education. Its basis being polyphony, each voice was able to sing from its own part without any reference to the others. Consequently, there was no trouble about cross-accents or rhythms, as each voice carried on its part, regardless of what the others might be doing.

The Madrigal was addressed mainly to nymphs and shepherdesses, the latter being personified in the name Phyllis. At the same time, it was the love-song of its period, and swooning lovers addressed reproaches to their fair maidens through its medium. A general study of madrigal verse suggests that the fair maidens always had their lovers in a state of frustration and were notable for inconsistency and waywardness. Others include numerous invocations to Nature.

The well-known *Triumphs of Oriana*, to which the leading composers of the day contributed, formed a panegyric of Queen Elizabeth I, each one ending with the refrain, "Then sang the shepherds and nymphs

of Diana, Long Live Fair Oriana''. The Queen doubtless saw through
most of the humbug, and accepted it for what it was worth, enjoying
the flattery, as would anyone else. In this collection the whole world,
mythological and otherwise, seems to be in a constant state of excite-
ment at the approach of the Queen.

Contemplative Madrigal style can be extremely beautiful with its
contrapuntal texture, as in "Fair is the rose" (Gibbons), while delineation by means of rapid tonguing of short syllables, as in "Sweet Suffolk
Owl", by Thomas Vautor, can be as true as anything obtainable on
the modern orchestra. The contrapuntal texture can be also humorous,
as "Fire! Fire!" by Thomas Morley shows.

Madrigals are often described as being "apt for voices and/or strings",
which means that they can be sung and played, or played without
being sung; this was not wildly exciting music for the players, but formed
one of the origins of instrumental chamber music.

EXAMPLES

"The Silver Swan" (Gibbons)   "All creatures now are merry-
"As Vesta was descending" (Weelkes)   minded" (Benet)[1]

BALLETS   Other similar works in the style are called "Ballets" (pronounced *balletts*), which were "apt for singing and dancing". These are
distinguished by the "Fa La's" which appear from time to time, the
dancing taking place at those moments, the singers thus being able to
disport themselves without special attention to diction. The technique
is the same as for the ordinary Madrigal.

EXAMPLES

"My Bonny Lass" (Morley)
"On the Plains" (Weelkes)

MELODRAMA   The original name for a recitation with musical
background, of which Richard Strauss's *Enoch Arden* is a notable and
standard example. It had no connection with its theatrical parallel,
and can refer to a short scene in an opera or play of any quality.

PART–SONG   The name given to a setting for ensemble singing
which may be harmonic throughout, with the tune at the top, or may
include alternating passages in the contrapuntal style. It differs from
the Madrigal in that a polyphonic basis is not necessary, and from the
Glee in that it is not necessarily for solo voices. It may be written for
two or more voices, for mixed voices, or for men or women alone. It
has no particular form of its own, and its composition relies entirely
upon the text.

---

[1] The line "The Nymphs are fa-la-la-ing" does not make it a Ballet.

It has always been popular since the time it supplanted the Glee; in the present century the enormous number of small choral societies which have sprung up all over the country, with their interest in Choral Competitive Festivals, has encouraged a great many composers to write Part-Songs. No list of examples could possibly be adequate. The reader should go into any publisher's showrooms and ask to see a few. After much experience of choirs at festivals, the writer can say that he has had most pleasure from these three songs, by widely different composers.

EXAMPLES

"The Lord is my Shepherd" (Schubert)—Female Voices
"O, breathe not his name" (Charles Wood)—Male Voices
"The Blue Bird" (Stanford)—Mixed Voices

Part-Songs by the following composers may be recommended for study: Stanford, Parry, Elgar, Charles Wood, Armstrong Gibbs, Bantock, Howells.

RECITATIVE An athematic passage in free declamatory style carrying narrative and conversational dialogue in an Opera or an Oratorio. There are two varieties:

1. Recitativo secco
2. Recitativo stromentato

1. RECITATIVO SECCO Originating in Italy at the end of the 16th century, it is a strict musical representation of the rise and fall of speech, the vocal line being supported by sustained or punctuating chords on the keyboard, intended to establish tonality, each line concluding with a strong cadence. Its description derives from the dry, snappy effect of Italian articulation. Its earliest exponents, Peri and Caccini, paid scant attention to its niceties, and regarded it as a means of getting round a difficulty.

Examples can be found in any Opera up to the period of Rossini and in any Oratorio up to the present day. It began to be superseded early in the 17th century by—

2. RECITATIVO STROMENTATO In this type of writing the accompaniment is played by the orchestra. Jean Baptiste Lully was the first composer to pay particular attention to syllabic emphasis, and took as much care over recitatives as he did over the writing of musical arias, etc. The style was perfected by Jean Philippe Rameau, whose recitativo stromentato is very like the Arioso. It is measured instead of being in free athematic rhythm, and is altogether melodic in quality. Examples can be found in any opera by these composers. Others can be found in Handel's *Messiah*.

On occasions composers have combined the two styles. In the *St.*

Matthew Passion, Bach writes recitativo secco for the narrative portions and for the human conversational passages, but the Voice of the Saviour is sustained by veiled string tone in the recitativo stromentato manner.

This particular style has been considerably extended, and may be said to have merged almost entirely into the lyrical and symphonic principles of Opera since the time of Wagner. Composers now carry their narratives and conversations along in continuous music, and it is often difficult to indicate with any certainty exactly where recitativo stromentato begins and ends. The pinnacle of this development was reached by Debussy in *Pelléas et Mélisande*, where his technique depends entirely upon the rise and fall of the syllables and completely eschews arias and ensemble numbers.

Arnold Schoenberg initiated his own particular *Sprechgesang*. This is a halfway measure between singing and speaking. It may be regarded as an offshoot of recitativo stromentato without claiming any musical affinity with it. It is most clearly demonstrated in Alban Berg's *Wozzeck*.

To-day composers introduce an isolated line of recitativo secco which relieves the ear from the strain of listening to a constant stream of music. On the other hand, the composer can find recitativo secco an easy way out of a difficulty. The best example of a compromise may be found in Charpentier's *Louise*, where the concept is almost entirely lyrical, and in Debussy's *Pelléas et Mélisande*, which is written in its own particular style, to which the description recitativo lyrico might be applied.

SERENATA   This is another name for a secular Cantata composed in honour of an individual or event, usually a Court or family birth-day. It has usually a mythological subject, and its style is such that it can be suitable for stage presentation, unlike the ordinary Cantata. Handel's *Acis and Galatea* is a good model of its kind. It often contained some symbolical flattery of the individual honoured. It flourished in Vienna in the 18th century, and Handel endeavoured to introduce it to England, but the Stuart habit of writing Festival Anthems had gained too firm a hold.

SONG   A setting of sacred or secular words, more often the latter, to be sung by a single voice with instrumental accompaniment. This is a general definition, and does not preclude the unaccompanied song which enjoyed a short vogue some years ago. There are various kinds of songs.

    1. Folk-Song   3. Ballad (or Drawing-room Song)
    2. Traditional Song   4. Art Song

    1. FOLK-SONG   It is impossible to say when the first folk-song came into being, for it was a spontaneous lyrical outburst on the part of some

obscure countryman which attracted the attention of others and remained fixed in the memories of all in that particular district. The
origin of the words is equally obscure. Often a curious line like "With
my roo-rum-ray, fol-the-diddle-doll", etc., appears, and these apparently
meaningless words have troubled musical authorities for years. It may
be suggested that they crept in when the singer could not remember
the original line, and that the jargon, fitting the music as it did,
was as good as any other. This is pure conjecture, of course. The
words are frequently coarse, but often extremely beautiful in their
simplicity.

The music comes under the heading of "Modal"; this is not to be
confused with the Gregorian Tone. The characteristic is a flattened
leading-note and any music containing this feature among others is
said to have a "folk-song flavour". The strongly national idiom of the
Folk-song identifies its country of origin. The differences between the
English Folk-song, the French Chanson Populaire and the German
Volkslied is apparent after two measures, and constant variety is found
in the regional versions. The wealth of a country's culture lies fundamentally in its Folk-songs.

2. TRADITIONAL SONG   Unlike the Folk-song, the Traditional Song is
not necessarily Modal, and in many cases the composer is known. The
song becomes traditional after a period of time, through strong associations. Songs like "Heart of Oak" and "The British Grenadiers" are
traditional.

3. BALLAD OR DRAWING-ROOM SONG   This has been dealt with
elsewhere.

4. ART SONG   This is a convenient name for a setting of poems which
have no Folk or Traditional associations. In France they are known as
"Mélodies", in Germany as "Lieder". Of the three terms, the French
appeared last, the first use of it being Berlioz' *Mélodies irlandaises* in
1830. Later the word "Romance" was applied to the sentimental effu-
sions of Gounod, but generally the term "mélodie" is used. The second
(Lieder) is distinguished by a great many German and Austrian composers, the term being applicable first to settings by Beethoven and
Schubert.

The Art Song may maintain the interest solely in the voice part,
the accompaniment being perfunctory, or the interest may be equally
divided. In a case like the beautiful *Morgen* of Richard Strauss, the
instrumental part is of even more importance than the vocal, the latter
appearing almost as a kind of commentary upon the mood set by the
former. With Debussy, voice and accompaniment are equally important.
There is no set form for songs, but a composer should not look upon
the composition of a song as something to be taken in hand lightly,
although many budding composers try to start their careers this way.
Songs by the following composers are recommended for study:

Songs	Mélodies	Lieder
Parry	Fauré	Wolf
Stanford	Roussel	Brahms
Ireland	Ropartz	Reger
Warlock	Debussy	Strauss
Moeran	Ravel	Schreker

One other type should be mentioned, and that is the School Song, which may be in unison or in two or more parts. This is necessarily straightforward, with diatonic melodies and reasonably easy accompaniments. The Unison Song for massed singing must be suitable for this purpose, and for this purpose only. Any attempt at turning it into a Solo or Art Song should fail if the true ideal is to be maintained. The Unison Song can be extremely stirring, the words having some spiritual uplift or moral purpose about them. They can be, however, and often are, of a quiet nature, but the contemplative text seems to call for part rather than unison singing. It is worth remarking that, while girl choirs enjoy the vigorous masculine type of Unison Song, boys abhor anything suggestive of sentimentality, and a study of the words is just as important as a scrutiny of the music. This is not often realised, and at choral festivals I have seen choirs of boys looking faintly ill and almost blushing at the effeminacy of the words they are perforce articulating.

ECCLESIASTICAL FORMS

ANTHEM This may be regarded as a natural evolution from the Motet but is wider in scope and resource. It can be accompanied or unaccompanied; but whereas the Motet is basically polyphonic, the unaccompanied Anthem is basically harmonic, the contrapuntal passages being quite short. Its constituent elements, therefore, are exactly the reverse of those of its forebear. It is no more necessary for the text of the Anthem to be in English than for that of the Motet to be in Latin.

The Anthem came "officially" into the English Liturgy when the Book of Common Prayer was revised during the reign of Charles II, in 1672, the rubric "In quires and places where they sing, here followeth the Anthem" being inserted in the Offices of Matins and Evensong.[1] There are three types of Anthem: (1) Full, (2) Solo, (3) Verse.

1. FULL ANTHEM This is sung throughout by the entire choir, and may be accompanied or unaccompanied. There may be a passage for men or for boys alone; unless this is marked expressly for solo voices, it remains a "chorus" and does not alter the category of the Anthem. An example of this can be found in Charles Wood's "Glorious and Powerful God", where the second verse is for men alone, in unison.

EXAMPLES

(a) Unaccompanied

"O Lord, the Maker of all things" (Henry VIII)[2]

"Remember not, Lord, our offences" (Purcell)

"Cry aloud and shout" (Croft)

"Cast me not away from Thy Presence" (S. S. Wesley)

"Glorious and powerful God" (Stanford)[3]

(b) Accompanied

"Zadok the Priest" (Handel)

"O Lord God, Thou strength" (Goss)

"Thou Judge of quick and dead" (S. S. Wesley)

"Wash me throughly" (S. S. Wesley)

2. SOLO ANTHEM This includes at least one passage of any length for solo voice. The passage will be accompanied, but the accompaniment need not be instrumental; it can be in the massed under-parts, as in Stanford's "O Living Will", where there is a treble solo at the words "A voice as unto him that hears", while the altos, tenors, and basses

---

[1] Some authorities maintain that this means "Hymn", Church composers taking advantage of the literal meaning of the word Anthem.

[2] Or so ran the picturesque legend until discredited by certain experts, who ascribe it to William Mundy.

[3] This is one of a set described as "Motets", but its harmonic basis gives it no academic claim to be so regarded.

maintain the harmony, entering with the same words a few beats behind. Almost a set form came into fashion during the Victorian era consisting of a chorus, a solo, and a closing chorus, the opening full section sometimes being an introduction and fugue, as in S. S. Wesley's "O give thanks", whose middle section is a model ecclesiastical solo.

The Solo Anthem reached its nadir in the Victorian era, when the general tone became highly sentimental and often reached that state known vulgarly as "sob-stuff". Composers sometimes divide their Solo Anthems into two sections, the first enunciating the solo, and the second repeating the same passage for S.A.T.B.

EXAMPLES

"Turn Thy Face from my sins" (Attwood)

"Lead, kindly light" (Stainer)

"It is high time to arise" (Barnby)

"And I saw another Angel" (Stanford)

3. VERSE ANTHEM   This is a more elaborate affair than the other two types. It includes one or more ensemble passages, together with one or more solos. The term "Verse" is used to denote these ensemble sections, and has no literary connotations.

The heyday of the Verse Anthem came at the moment of its re-introduction in England.[1] Charles II, when in exile, had listened to the music of Lully at the Court of Louis XIV. He did not intend to tolerate austerity in the Church services and sent Pelham Humfrey to study under Lully. Humfrey is said to have travelled in Italy as well, and upon his return the leading composers of the time set themselves to study the "new-fangled ideas". Dr. John Blow, the foremost of these composers, in turn imparted the technique to his pupil, Henry Purcell. Verse Anthems soon became almost miniature Cantatas, and in some cases are even longer than some of Bach's. The tradition was handed down to William Croft, Maurice Greene, and William Boyce. The Chandos Anthems of Handel were most like the Bach Cantatas by reason of their length and instrumental scope. Later elaboration of the tradition came with the anthems of S. S. Wesley, whose *The Wilderness* has all the elements of a Cantata. The Hanoverian composers marred their otherwise stirring fugal anthems by writing dreary wastes of vocal trios, in which two parts move in unbroken thirds while the third voice remains static. Some of the fugal choruses, as in "God is gone up", by William Croft, exhale a bluff English atmosphere.

The Verse Anthem gradually became reduced in length and scope in accordance with the increasing speed of life, and to-day, when people can no longer spend nearly all the morning or evening in church, emphasis is placed upon directness of expression. Probably the maximum

---

[1] The Elizabethan composers wrote them in the first place, but they went temporarily out of fashion soon afterwards.

length tolerable to-day is that of Parry's great Coronation Anthem, "I was glad" (excluding the special Coronation section), which contains a beautiful passage for mixed Quartet (or Semi-chorus). The Verse Anthem naturally offers the composer much scope for expression, and the Stuart composers were not slow to use it dramatically. Some of the Anthems of this period, and of the earlier Hanoverians, show a remarkable insight into dramatic feeling and instinct which is never theatrical, yet suggests that had the composers been connected with Opera and the dramatic stage (as was Purcell) the history of English Opera might have been a less depressing one.

The musical layout of the Verse Anthem has no set form and it may be useful to study the general outline of a particular one:

O Sing unto the Lord (Purcell)

Introductory Symphony	44 bars
Bass Solo (Recitativo stromentato)	
"O sing unto the Lord a new song"	5 bars
Chorus (Fugato)	
"Hallelujah"	15 bars
Bass Solo (Recitativo stromentato)	
"Sing unto the Lord all the whole earth"	9 bars
Chorus (Chordal)	
"Hallelujah"	15 bars
Ritornello	28 bars
Mixed Verse Quartet (Fugato)	
Part One: "Sing unto the Lord and praise His Name" .	10 bars
Part Two: "Be telling of His salvation from day to day" .	10 bars
Bass Solo (Recitativo stromentato)	
"Declare His honour unto the heathen: and His wonders unto all people"	12 bars
Chorus (Chordal)	
"Glory and worship are before Him"	2 bars
Ritornello	2 bars
"Glory and worship are before Him"	2 bars
Ritornello	2 bars
"Power and honour are in His sanctuary" . . .	5 bars
Verse (Two Voices) on Ground Bass	
Part One: "The Lord is great and cannot worthily be praised; He is more to be feared than all gods" . .	22 bars
Part Two: "As for all the gods of the heathen, they are but idols; but it is the Lord that made the heavens" . .	19 bars
Ritornello	36 bars

Mixed Verse Quartet and Chorus
  Verse: "O worship the Lord in the beauty of holiness"   .   5 bars
  Chorus: "O worship the Lord in the beauty of holiness: let
    the whole earth stand in awe of Him"   .   .   .   . 15 bars

Bass Solo and Chorus
  Solo: "Tell it out among the heathen that the Lord is King"   2 bars
  Chorus: "The Lord is King"   .   .   .   .   .   .   2 bars
  Solo: "and that it is He that hath made the round world so
    sure that it cannot be moved"   .   .   .   .   . 4 bars
  Chorus: "it is He that hath made the round world so sure
    that it cannot be moved"   .   .   .   .   .   . 4 bars
  Solo: "and how that He shall judge the people righteously" 4 bars
  Chorus: "He shall judge the people righteously"   .   . 5 bars

Mixed Verse, Quartet and Chorus (Fugato)
  Verse: "Allelujah"   .   .   .   . 10 bars
  Chorus: "Allelujah"   .   .   .   . 12 bars
  Ritornello   .   .   .   . 8 bars
  Chorus: "Allelujah! Amen"   .   .   .   .   .   . 20 bars

EXAMPLES

"I beheld, and lo!" (Blow)   "By the Waters of Babylon" (Boyce)
"Prepare ye the way of the Lord"   "Ascribe unto the Lord" (S. S.
  (Wise)   Wesley)
"Ascribe unto the Lord" (Travers)   "Praise the Lord, my soul" (Wesley)
"O where shall wisdom be found?"   "It came even to pass" (Ouseley)
  (Boyce)   "The Wilderness" (Goss)

CANTATA (SACRED)   In contrast to the Toccata, which implies a piece to be "touched" on the keyboard, the Cantata implies a piece to be sung either by a single voice or by any number of voices with accompaniment for organ or orchestral instruments. It has a succession of movements. The Sacred Cantata can either tell a short story, in which case it becomes a miniature Oratorio, or can consist of a number of ensemble and solo movements which comment upon some portion of the Scripture applicable to the Gospel or Second Lesson appointed for the day. It was part of Bach's routine work to compose a weekly Cantata, and he wrote more than two hundred of them, sometimes making use of movements from older works.

There is no hard and fast rule as regards the musical shape of a Cantata; this is dictated entirely by the quality of the text. Broadly speaking, the classical Cantata opens with an orchestral introduction to a chorus, followed by a recitative and solo or ensemble number, and a final chorus usually founded upon a chorale; this is the minimum structure, and many are much longer. The seasons and festivals of the Church have supplied innumerable composers with excuses for writing Cantatas, the most insidious being, apparently, that of the Harvest which, by reason of its symbolism, has been responsible for much musical bathos.

From Bach to Stainer is a far cry, in more than one sense, but Stainer produced a work whose original purpose has been forgotten in the general regret at its banality. *The Crucifixion* was composed in order that village and small town choirs could have something to sing of less magnitude than the *St. Matthew Passion*; but while aiming at simplicity, Stainer became sentimental and cadence-bound; nearly every sentence ends with a full close. Between the lives of these two, and since, many composers have written admirable works which form good material for any choral society which has no qualms at singing sacred words in a secular building. There is a field here for the modern composer who does not spend his life within the confines of an organ loft.

It is difficult to make a choice from the two hundred-odd Cantatas of Bach, and in any case the list must be short.

EXAMPLES

Bach

"Praise our God who reigns in Heaven" "God's own time is the best"
"Sleepers, Wake!" Each separate part of the *Christ-*
"The Sages of Sheba" *mas Oratorio*

Later examples

The Song of Miriam (Schubert) *Lauda Sion* (Mendelssohn)
Advent Hymn (Schumann)

The words of a Sacred Cantata need not be biblical, and a balance has been found between sacred and secular by using words with sacred implications. Composers commissioned to write works for the Three Choirs Festivals find this happy medium, and a work like *Blest Pair of Sirens*, by Parry, is at home in a sacred building as well as a concert hall. This, like many others, is in one continuous movement for chorus alone, and differs from what has been discussed as a kind of liturgical Cantata. Care should be taken before the commencement of composition to see that an unliturgical or unbiblical text is fully suit-able in the eyes of ecclesiastical authority. Let the composer remember the case of *Belshazzar's Feast*, by Sir William Walton, which was rejected for performance at a Three Choirs Festival owing to the pagan shouts of praise in the first part. It is not so many years ago that qualms were felt in the same circles over the Baal choruses in Mendelssohn's *Elijah*.

A composer seeking a text for a sacred Cantata can still find ample scope in the Psalms of David. Out of one hundred and fifty psalms there are still a good many unset to music.

F

EXAMPLES

By the Waters of Babylon (Goetz)	*To the Name above Every Name* (Bax)
De Profundis (Parry)	*A Hymn to God the Father* (Bainton)
Toward the Unknown Region (Vaughan Williams)	*In Glorious Freedom* (Brent-Smith)

CHANT There are two kinds of Chant to which the Psalms and Canticles are sung—Gregorian and Anglican. The former is known as a "Tone" which, in general, bears the description of Plainchant or Plainsong. The so-called Gregorian Tones by Pope Gregory were an extension of the earlier Ambrosian Modes, Pope Gregory adding four, called "Plagal", to the original or Authentic four. These Gregorian Tones have come to be regarded as the perquisite of the Roman Catholic Communion. This error has arisen because for many years the Anglican Communion has used its own special variety of chant. To-day many Anglican churches use Plainsong, and the system is, as it has always been, general property.

Each Tone has alternative "Endings", and the set of eight has had one added—namely, the Tonus Peregrinus.[1] The effect is one of monotony, but of dignity.

The Anglican Chant is derived from the Gregorian Tone. It is divided, as in the Gregorian Tone, into three strains—Intonation, Recitation, Mediation. The chief difference is that, while the Gregorian is flexible, the Anglican is rigid, although this difficulty has been largely overcome by modern "pointing"—the method of singing psalms to Anglican chants.

There are four kinds of Anglican Chant, Single, Double, Triple, and Quadruple. These are used in accordance with the grouping of the verses of the Psalm; triple and quadruple groupings are rare. The double grouping does not always balance, the odd verse being sung to the second part of the chant. This invariably sounds clumsy, and many of the newest psalters obviate it by telescoping two verses into one.

Anglican pointing is a tradition peculiar to every church, and the effect of antiphonal singing is always impressive when sung properly. If the chant happens to be a bad one the effect can be exasperating—Dvořák was sent nearly mad by the "constant repetition of a bad tune". On the other hand, many chants are extremely beautiful. It is customary to change the chant when the spirit of the psalm concerned requires it.

CHORALE A type of metrical song of praise common to the Lutheran and Old Catholic Churches of Germany. It is sung slowly, with a pause at the end of each line, regardless of the sense of the words.

---

[1] I cannot omit reference to the directive issued by a newly-appointed Dean of a cathedral who asked the organist to use single rather than double chants, as he did not want the services to be unduly drawn-out.

Originally an Interlude was played on the organ between each line; this custom has now been moderated, and the Interlude is played between each verse. It allows the organist some opportunity for extemporisation on a small scale. The slow speed of the music also enables him to vary the harmonies from verse to verse, since the singing is in unison. J. S. Bach was roundly taken to task for playing such complicated harmonies that the Faithful were unable to concentrate upon the tune.

Bach's *Passions* include a great number of chorales designed to allow the congregation to take a vocal part in commenting upon the situations in the narrative. This affords relief to the otherwise continual listening, and there are few moments more moving than those when a large audience joins in the singing of such broad tunes. Bach harmonised each one with harmony expressive of the text; consequently there are several harmonisations of the same tune. These afford striking examples of how to obtain contrasting expression by simple progressions.

Attention should be given to those chorales in Bach's cantatas which have orchestral interludes between each line, like that concluding Part Two of the *Christmas Oratorio*—"With all Thy Hosts, O Lord, we sing" —where the interludes consist of the quasi-pipe music previously heard in the "Pastoral" Symphony.

HYMN A metrical song of praise sometimes confused with the chorale, with which it has little in common.

Hymn-tunes are square in character; many old examples begin and end each line with a long note. This custom has returned to a certain extent; but if a breath be taken at the end of each line, utter rubbish can result, the following being common instances: "My God, I love Thee, not because", "Awaked from sleep we fall", and "The bleeding martyrs, they".[1] The hymn-tune is usually expressive of the first line of the hymn to which it applies, composers seemingly gaining their impulse from this alone and not from the whole hymn. Consequently, it happens only too often that all the laws of syllabic emphasis are defied, and the notes go up instead of down, and vice versa; a classic example of this can be found in Barnby's tune to "For all the Saints", where the points of emphasis of the lines "Thou in the darkness *drear*, their one true Light" fall in the wrong places.

The present-day tendency is to avoid the square metrical principle and to compose broad, swinging tunes which can be altered in those places where there would otherwise be faulty accentuation. Vaughan Williams's "For all the Saints" and "Hail thee, Festival Day" are good instances of this.

---

[1] While there is the Choirboys' authority for "Another year of leaning" (on their desks).

MASS The form of service known in Churches, other than the Roman Catholic, under the name of Eucharist or Holy Communion. The sequence is as follows:

Kyrie Eleison	Credo in Unum Deum
Christe Eleison	Sanctus
Kyrie Eleison	Benedictus qui venit
Gloria in Excelsis	Agnus Dei

The Kyrie[1] is sung nine times in all, each invocation being repeated twice. The music may be simple and liturgical, accompanied or unaccompanied, or it may be elaborate, its musical ambitions far outreaching its liturgical suitability. In the strictly liturgical sense the music is straightforward, that for the Credo being the same upon each occasion in order that the faithful may take a vocal part. The music in this case is known as "Plainsong" and is in unison, with austere organ accompaniment. The polyphonic Masses of the 16th century are equally liturgical; but here the faithful recite the words to themselves and then allow their minds to be elevated by the music. This applies equally to settings with organ or orchestral accompaniment.

Such Masses as that in B minor by Bach and that in D by Beethoven for soloists, chorus, and full orchestra were never intended for liturgical use. These works take on the manner of the Oratorio and form a complete musical performance in themselves. Their scope and resource are manifold, and the composer is under no restrictions as to repetition of words or length of performance.

EXAMPLES

(a) Simple Liturgical

Missa de Angelis   *Missa Aeterna Christi Munera* (unison version)

(b) Liturgical

Mass for Three Voices (Byrd)   *Missa Papae Marcelli* (Palestrina)
Mass for Four Voices (Byrd)   Mass in G minor (Vaughan Williams)

(c) Extra-Liturgical

Any by Haydn, Mozart, Schubert

Included in the service but not necessarily in the musical setting are the Introit, Gradual, Alleluia, Prose, Sequence, Offertory, and Communion. There are too many exceptions to allow of any definite statement.

---

[1] It is customary to refer to each movement by the first line or even first word of the text.

On the Continent, Sunday Low Mass is accompanied by an organ recital, the service proceeding in the ordinary way while the organist plays suitable music, thus setting the right spiritual mood. The pieces are arranged as follows:

Introit	Communion
Offertoire	Grand Chœur
Élévation	

The last always sounds a note of triumph and dispels the deep mystical atmosphere engendered by the Liturgy.

MOTET A setting of sacred or quasi-sacred words to unaccompanied polyphonic music, the basic polyphony not forbidding an occasional harmonic passage, should the text require it, as in Byrd's "Bow Thine Ear", at the words "Zion, Thy Zion, is wasted and brought low", and the same composer's "Sing joyfully", where square chordal writing aptly illustrates the text—"Blow the trumpet in the new moon". Sectarian purists maintain that unless the words are in Latin, the work is not a Motet. This is pure nonsense, since it is the musical style and not the language of the text which is the deciding factor. Orlando Gibbons's "Hosanna to the Son of David" is just as much a Motet as Palestrina's "Tu es Petrus".

EXAMPLES

"Spem in alium" (Tallis)—in forty parts
"O Bone Jesu" (Carver)—in nineteen parts
"Haec Dies" (Byrd)
"Hosanna to the Son of David" (Weelkes)
"Singer dem Herrn" (Bach)
"O Lord, look down from Heaven" (Battishill)
"In Exitu Israel" (S. Wesley)
"Exaltate Deo" (S. Wesley)
"There is an old belief" (Parry)

The name Motet is occasionally given to instrumental pieces in the polyphonic manner, designed for church performance.

ORATORIO Originating in Italy in the 16th century, Oratorio obtained a firm hold in England during the time of Handel. It constitutes a dramatic performance without action, the narrative moments being expounded in recitative. The elements are choruses, vocal solos, vocal ensembles and instrumental interludes, etc. The subjects are sacred, and the present-day tendency is to broaden the outlook while keeping a certain religious aspect to the fore. The Oratorio manner, however, is slowly growing out of favour, and modern composers, especially those in France, lean to the Mystère; the Cantata still maintains its popularity in this country. The essentially religious basis was broken by Haydn when he composed *The Seasons*, but this still keeps in touch with sacred matters through choruses of thanksgiving—"Be propitious, bounteous Heaven", for example—which justify its description as Oratorio.

Oratorios are noted for their fugal choruses, and these have hardly been bettered since the days of Handel. The Bach *Passions* are sometimes described as Oratorios, but are in fact a form in themselves. The musical layout has been greatly extended in recent times, and Honegger has substituted spoken dialogue, behind music, for the older recitative. The love for Oratorio displayed through many years of English musical history has always mystified foreign visitors, who feel that we regard the form as a kind of Church service. Indeed, so firmly had the impression been formed that when Camille Saint-Saëns, the prolific French composer, was invited to compose a work for the Three Choirs Festival of 1912, he thought that our taste was limited to quasi-Handelian Oratorio. He composed a long and tedious work upon traditional lines, called *The Promised Land*, which scored an instantaneous failure for this very reason.

The proper home for Oratorio is a church, but for economic reasons the majority of performances take place in concert halls. This is in accordance with the policy of Handel, who originated the practice of performing Oratorios in the theatre. There is something incongruous in Handel's *Messiah*, for example, being treated in this secular manner, and, although tradition forbids applause for this particular work, that tradition is usually disregarded. On the other hand, an Oratorio like *Israel in Egypt* is quite suitable for performance in the concert hall, and the same may be said of Mendelssohn's *Elijah*. It appears as though the Old Testament stories were more adaptable in this respect than those of the New Testament, and certainly Mendelssohn's *St. Paul* and Liszt's *Christus* have a more suitable *milieu* in the church. In the present century, Elgar's *The Apostles* and *The Kingdom* are really suited only to the church; but *The Dream of Gerontius* fits in any setting. This is peculiar, because the heavy mysticism of the book and of the music would seem to be out of place under concert conditions.

There are many examples of Oratorios, and it is useless to particularise in many instances, particularly in the case of Handel. The reader's attention may be drawn, however, to certain less familiar works which illustrate various points of origin and extension, some of which are, admittedly, not easily available.

Jeptha (Carissimi)
Christmas Oratorio (Schutz)
Saul (Handel)
The Last Judgement (Spohr)
The Childhood of Christ (Berlioz)
The Love Feast of the Apostles (Wagner)
Les Béatitudes (Franck)
The Legend of St. Elizabeth (Liszt)
The Rose of Sharon (Mackenzie)

Judith (Parry)[1]
Job (Parry)
Christ in the Wilderness (Bantock)
King David (Honegger)
Sancta Civitas (Vaughan Williams)
Jacob's Ladder (Schoenberg)
Das Unaufhörliche (Hindemith)
Apocalypse (Françaix)
Jonah (Berkeley)

REQUIEM MASS The form of service commemorating the departed. It does not follow the ordinary sequence of the Mass, as the Gloria and Credo are omitted and other movements are interpolated. The sequence is:

Requiem aeternam dona eis (Introit)
Te decet hymnus, Deus in Sion
Kyrie Eleison
Dies irae
Tuba mirum spargens
Rex tremendae majestatis
Recordare, Jesu pie
Confutatis maledictis

Lacrimosa dies illa
Domine Jesu Christe (Offertorium)
Hostias et preces tibi, Domine
Sanctus
Benedictus qui venit
Agnus Dei
Lux aeterna luceat eis, Domine

This is ordinarily sung to Plainsong, but composers have often been attracted to the dramatic character of the text and have set it to elaborate music for soloists, chorus, and orchestra, in the oratorio manner, which is not suitable for liturgical purposes. Many of these great works are theatrical to a degree, and it is interesting to notice those composers who have been impelled by the dramatic element rather than by any spiritual belief in the message.[2]

Mozart (much of it composed by Süssmayer)
Liszt
Verdi
Berlioz

Fauré
Ropartz
Duruflé

---

[1] Parry himself described this work as "comical, old-fashioned stuff", but it has certain qualities which commend it. These include the "Lament of Manasseh", the March, "Behold ye the watchmen on the walls; is it peace?" and particularly the dramatic effect of Judith's outburst, "Ho, ye!" which is a masterstroke unexpected from an anti-operatic composer like Parry.

[2] Berlioz said he wished his *Tuba mirum* to resound "from cemetery to cemetery".

SERVICE   When the Liturgy appeared in English for the first time, the term Service was applied to the musical settings of the daily offices, the setting being known as "So-and-So in D" or whatever key the music is in. Composers are said to write "Morning", "Evening", and "Communion Services".

Holy Communion   In the First Prayer-Book [1549] the sequence was maintained as in the Roman Mass. It was found, however, that this arrangement was not altogether satisfactory, as it meant that there were three long stretches of music in succession. More important still, was the feeling that the service itself lacked climax, since there was no final act of thanksgiving. The Gloria in Excelsis, therefore, was placed at the end in the Second Prayer-Book of [1553.] The original Ninefold Kyrie was removed after the introduction of the Ten Commandments, and a response was written for use with the first nine, followed by a particular one after the Tenth, this embracing the entire decalogue. Nowadays the Ninefold Kyrie has been restored in many churches, and the Two Great Commandments are substituted for the Ten. In some cases the original Greek words are used, in others the English translation. Many churches, however, use the Response originally appointed for use "after the Tenth".

The music in the English Use is either congregational or choral, but it is often customary to use the same setting of the Creed in order that the Faithful may make a vocal profession of their Faith, the other movements being choral. In this case the music is always extremely simple, a plainsong setting being used, very often that by John Merbecke, or some modern setting which, like the *Folk Mass* of Martin Shaw, is in a plainsong idiom.

The choral settings range from easy diatonic music for village and small town choirs to the more elaborate versions with organ accompaniment for large town and cathedral choirs. Polyphonic settings are used in the two latter centres, English Church Music having some notable examples of them. A few English churches use the less elaborate settings by the classical composers (e.g. Schubert in G) sung in translation; but this is seldom really satisfactory, since the text has then to be fitted to the music, and not the other way round. On certain great festivals these churches use an orchestra instead of the organ, this being a direct reflection of pre-organ days, when the accompaniment was provided by a nondescript orchestra consisting of cornet, bassoon (serpent), and bass viol, and anything else which happened to be available.

As far as can be ascertained no one has as yet composed a setting to English words of the same scope as those by Bach and Beethoven to the Latin. This is mainly because the English Eucharist in the native tongue has a sense of intimacy about it which is precluded by the theatrical nature of the Roman Mass.

EXAMPLES

(a) Simple Unison

Merbecke   Howells in G
Folk Mass (Martin Shaw)   Bairstow in E flat

(b) Alla capella

The Great Service (Byrd)   Charles Wood in the Phrygian Mode
Gibbons in F   Vaughan Williams

(c) Accompanied

Lloyd in E flat   Stanford in B flat
Harwood in A flat

Matins This is one of the Daily Offices, and consists of Prayers, Psalms, and Canticles. The Canticles usually set to music are Te Deum, Benedictus or Jubilate. The Jubilate has almost fallen out of use since its presence forbids any reference in the Office to the Incarnation. It is used, however, when the words of the Benedictus come into the narrative of the Second Lesson. At one time composers wrote settings for the Venite, but this never became established, and it is now invariably sung to a chant. Most churches with an advisedly congregational intention use chants for the Canticles.

Evensong This is another of the Daily Offices. Its Order is the same as that for Matins. The Canticles usually set to music are Magnificat, Nunc Dimittis or Cantate Domino, Deus misereatur. The alternatives are used when the words of the former appear in the narrative of the Second Lesson.

The history of English Church Music shows a decline from a high standard to a subsequent revival. From the polyphonic ideas of the 16th century to the Cantata-like principle of Purcell, on to the dull and unimaginative settings of the Hanoverian composers, through the dreadful sentimentalities of the Victorians, to the dignity and common sense of the Edwardians and present-day Elizabethans. The Hanoverians excelled in canonic device and technical prowess—to the complete exclusion of feeling and sentiment. Mistaking the true meaning of this last word, the Victorians, in the persons of Stainer and Barnby, endeavoured to restore the situation by becoming sentimental, and although there were several exceptions, notably S. S. Wesley and the Rev. George Garrett, the standard reached a low level of meretricious bathos. It fell to Stanford to restore the Service to its original dignity, and although nearly every organist and choirmaster feels constrained to express himself in some key or other for his own choir to sing, the standard has been maintained through enlightened direction.

It is customary to deride the Victorians, and rightly so; but the pendulum has swung too far and the influence they exercised in revitalising spiritual values has been overlooked amid the masses of inferior music. These composers elaborated and underlined many perfectly plain statements, which required no elaboration or delineation. New conventions crept in. The canonic and fugal traditions of the Hanoverians went from bad to worse, and it became fashionable "to fugue" the response in the Gloria—sometimes with ludicrous results. Thus Sir Joseph Barnby announced in the key of E that "As it was, it was in the beginning", a theological pronouncement described by Tovey as "the chorister's Fortieth Article". It was given to the three composers already mentioned to restore reason, and Wesley (in E), Garrett (in D), and Stanford (in B flat) set the models for all time.

The rights and wrongs of English Services can be examined in the following examples:

EXAMPLES

The Boke of Common Praier Noted (Merbecke)
Tallis in D
The Great Service (Byrd)
Gibbons in F
Farrant in G minor
Childe in G
Purcell in D minor
King in C
Nares in F
Walmisley in D minor

Wesley in E
Stainer in A
Barnby in E
Stanford in B flat
Stanford in G
Garrett in D
Noble in B minor
Harwood in A flat
Lloyd in E flat

Attention should be given to the Evening Service by Stanford, in G, which reveals original qualities—the Magnificat is set for treble solo with organ and choral accompaniment. The treble represents the Blessed Virgin, while the organ accompaniment suggests a spinning-wheel whose whir forms a background to the comments of the believers. The Nunc Dimittis is set for baritone solo representing the aged Simeon, with choral commentary. This is achieved with no theatrical effect, and the Service remains unique.[1]

Elaboration in Church Music must be kept within limits, for the music must always be expressive, technique being entirely subservient to the spirit of the text.

---

[1] This setting is recommended to those who produce Nativity Plays.

SUBJECT INDEX

Rockliff Music Books

MUSICAL TRENDS IN THE 20TH CENTURY by Norman Demuth

"*Can be warmly recommended as a sort of Baedeker to the many bewildered travellers who are now trying to take their bearings. How many trends there have been in music during the last fifty years will perhaps surprise the casual reader—he will find Mr. Demuth an excellent guide.*"—Ernest Newman in The Sunday Times.

"*This is incisive, often fearless and quite original criticism, springing from wide knowledge and real insight . . . for the professional musician or critic a thorough study of this book is, if under 30, a necessity; if over 30, a duty.*"—Yorkshire Post.

Cloth Demy 8vo.　　　*45 portraits, 131 musical examples.*　　　35s. net.

U.S.A.: The Macmillan Co.

VINCENT D'INDY—Champion of Classicism, 1851–1931 by Norman Demuth

"*Sincere and bound to leave those who have hitherto judged d'Indy without knowing him with a new respect for a noble musical personality.*"—Eric Blom in The Observer.

"*It is a pleasure to be able to welcome, at last, an authoritative book, in English and by an Englishman, on d'Indy, a great man underestimated here. Mr. Demuth has produced a book long overdue. All we could want more is more d'Indy. This little book will have no little share in helping to an understanding of a great mind difficult and almost too consciously idealistic.*"—Tempo.

Chapters include: Vincent d'Indy—the Man; The Teacher; The Composer—General Survey, Aesthetic, Technique, Design; d'Indy and the Lyric Stage.

With numerous musical examples, list of compositions, bibliography, portrait frontispiece and index.

Cloth Crown 8vo.　　　　　　　　　　9s. 6d. net.

FRITZ KREISLER by Louis P. Lochner

"*This painstaking biography.*"—Richard Capell in The Daily Telegraph.

"*One cannot imagine more skilful bookmaking than this life of one of the greatest and most beloved artists in musical history.*"—Musical Opinion.

With an "illustrated" catalogue of Kreisler's musical works and arrangements; a list of his gramophone recordings, etc., bibliography of references to Kreisler and his background in books and periodicals, 15 plates, including early portraits and pictures of Kreisler's famous violins.

Cloth Demy 8vo.　　　　　　　　　　25s. net.

U.S.A.: The Macmillan Co.

BENJAMIN BRITTEN   Edited by Donald Mitchell and Hans Keller

By a group of specialists including: Lord Harewood, Peter Pears, Dr. H. F. Redlich, George Auric, Joan Chissell, Paul Hamburger, Erwin Stein, Norman del Mar, Arthur Oldham, Boyd Neel, Imogen Holst, William Mann, Lennox Berkeley and George Malcolm. It is fully illustrated with numerous musical examples and contains a chronological list of works, bibliography and a critical discography by Desmond Shawe-Taylor.

Demy 8vo.   *13 pages of plates, over 200 musical examples.*   *30s. net.*

VIOLINS AND VIOLINISTS   by Franz Farga (*2nd Imp.*)

Translated by Egon Larsen. With a special chapter on English Violin Makers by E. W. Lavender, Editor of *The Strad*.

"*. . . will make all its readers ever grateful . . . shows a great deal of insight and research.*"—*Connoisseur*.

"*Truly a wonderful book, which every violinist should possess.*"—*Music Teacher*.

Cloth Demy 8vo.   138 half-tone illustrations and diagrams. A Collectors' Book Club Choice.   *30s. net.*

U.S.A.: The Macmillan Co.

VIOLINISTS OF TODAY   by Donald Brook (*3rd Imp.*)

"*Ideal volume . . . Well written, full of 'meat,' is well produced, and illustrated. It will be welcomed by many and should have a wide sale.*"—*The Schoolmaster*.

Cloth Large Cr. 8vo.   *28 Portraits.*   *16s. net.*

U.S.A.: The Macmillan Co.

MASTERS OF THE KEYBOARD   by Donald Brook
(*5th Imp.*)

"*Well-informed observations on the technique of piano playing with interesting biographical material.*"—*Manchester Evening News*.

Cloth Demy 8vo.   *35 plates.*   *16s. net.*

U.S.A.: The Macmillan Co.

COMPANION TO OPERA   by Donald Brook

"*Excellent . . . One of the most complete and up-to-date books of its kind.*"—*Yorkshire Evening News*.

Cloth Demy 8vo.   *63 Art Plates.*   *18s. net.*

COMPOSERS' GALLERY   by Donald Brook
(*2nd Ed. 3rd Imp*)

"*Composers' Gallery will be welcomed by music lovers and the larger public throughout the civilised world.*"—*Sir Granville Bantock*.

"*. . . a most competent survey.*"—*Compton Mackenzie*.

Cloth Demy 8vo.   *41 Art Plates.*   *18s. net.*

A-63-48A